Table of Contents

Introduction

Years ago when I went to go from building static webpages to a using a system like WordPress I needed to find a book on the subject, and there were plenty. My problem was that all of them either showed me step by step how to get the site up and running, and then stopped there. Or started out editing the PHP code and got more advanced from there.

I could find virtually no middle ground. What I wanted and needed was a book that started out showing me how to get off the ground and then built on that enough to give me a reasonably secure and usable website. These were nowhere to be found.

To make matters worse, there were some books that discussed installing and using WordPress and others that talked about using WordPress.com. What was the difference and why wouldn't anyone talk about both?

Why a book when WordPress has an excellent help system built right in? Two reasons: I like to get a jump start on new things by reading a book from start to finish as it gives me a great overall knowledge that I can then expand on using the help system, and it gives me the ability to learn without having to be online or even on a computer when I want to read.

Being a writer this "flipped that switch" that said I should just write the book I need myself. This is fantastic since it forces me to do all the research and work to learn what I wanted to know in the first place, and then figure out how best to pass this information on to the reader. There is no better way to learn than by doing this in my opinion, so off we go.

My goal is to take you from not knowing what WordPress is and only knowing what a website is from the end user's point of view, and then educating you into being able to install, secure and maintain a fully interactive website by reading only one book.

If you are looking for customizing the code of your themes, this is not the book for you. I will be putting much more emphasis on all the things you need for the website to work on a day to day basis instead of how to shift your icon over two pixels.

The focus of my website designs are simplicity for both the user and admin. I want as little work as possible. Tools that I use need to automate processes as much as possible so my workload is as light as possible. Heck, I am a writer and have no desire to administrate websites all day long. Most of the website admins I know don't want to do that all day long either because it is usually tedious work.

Simple, effective, fast and requiring as little interaction with the admin as possible. Those are my goals.

The book is divided into sections based on what you need to do. The first of those lays the foundation by discussing what a website is, what WordPress is and how those work together.

The second section walks you through installing WordPress from scratch using two different methods.

The third section takes you through virtually every screen and option in a default installation of WordPress and explains the functions to you.

The forth section presents topics such as security, backups, migration, translations and more to help you actually get your website moving forward.

The fifth section gives you places to go for more information, provides both a glossary and index, and then finally shows you some other titles by the author you might like.

If there is anything you like, don't like, disagree with, etc. please do not hesitate to come by my website at www.allans-stuff.com and drop me a line. I am always pleased to hear from my readers and constructive criticism, either good or bad, is always welcome.

On with the show!

Using this book

In this book I use some terminology and conventions that I want to point out right up front so you don't get confused. The first convention is navigation and it works like this:

Settings>General>Site Title

This refers to a location you can get to by clicking on Settings (1) and then clicking on General (2) and finally on the page that is displayed should be something with a label of Site Title (3) as shown in the image below.

If you have read other books on WordPress they may refer to everything you see after logging in to your WordPress site as the dashboard. My reading of the official Codex (documentation) seems to say that the dashboard is merely the large screen on the right that displays a lot of boxes such as Welcome to WordPress, At a Glance and Quick Draft when you first log into your administration screen.

Following the codex I refer to the entire screen as the administration screen with the navigation menu down the left hand side, the toolbar across the top, and the large portion called the work area on the right the display area as shown in the following image:

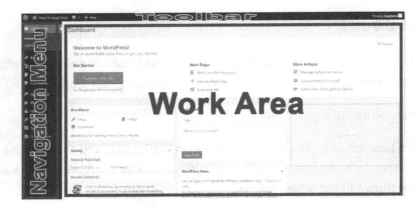

I assume that you will be reading the book from beginning to end and therefore there are things in later sections which refer back to previous sections for their explanations. If you choose to skip ahead you may miss some of the discussion.

A great example of this is when I discuss pages I spend almost no time on the editing screen for pages except to say it is virtually identical to the editing screen for posts discussed earlier in the book. I did not see the need to repeat pages and pages of information on something that is for all intents, identical.

This is also true when I am discussing the WordPress.com interface. I do not spend much time on discussing the terms used in this interface such as posts, pages, comments, widgets, etc. because all of those terms have already been discussed in the preceding section on full WordPress installations.

When looking at the screenshots I show you may notice that I do not always include the entire screen. I tend to include what is needed for you to understand what I am showing you and nothing more. This saves space in the book as well as brings your attention to the part of the screen where it needs to be instead of looking all over trying to find what I am talking about. Keep this in mind when you see partial screenshots.

When I talk about pressing keys such as Ctrl+C what I am saying is you need to press and HOLD the Crtl key on the keyboard and then press the C key, then finally release both keys.

Section 1: The basics

Before you jump in and try to set up your own WordPress website from scratch there are some basic things we need to cover. It is important for you to understand the building blocks and underpinnings of what we are trying to do, at least to a small degree, so that we have something to build on. You certainly wouldn't start building a house with the roof, would you?

It is also important that we both refer to the same thing by the same name. If you call something one thing and I call it another, then it will be quite a bit more difficult for me to get you where you want to be. I have some customers who genuinely think that a web browser *is* the internet. While their belief in that certainly doesn't hurt them, it would absolutely hurt us trying to converse about websites, ftp programs, and hosting services.

I am not talking about learning PHP or HTML code here, or learning to build your own web server, just some basic terminology and functionality. You probably already know most of this but it never hurts to make sure.

You may find that I use terms that other people tend to use different terms, which is fine. A website hosting company is the same thing as a hosting provider which can also be called just a web host. We only need to concern ourselves right now with being consistent within the book. You can always choose the variation of the term you want to use later.

Don't worry, this is a very small section and it won't take you long at all to blow through it so we can get to the good stuff.

1.1 What is a website?

Before we get into detail on WordPress we need to understand what a website is and how it basically functions.

There are three components to a typical website: the domain name, the web host and the website files.

The domain name is the name you see at the top of your browser, for example www.yahoo.com. I have several but the ones most closely associated with this book are www.paperbirdtek.com because it is computer related and www.allans-stuff.com because that is where I put information on all the books I write, regardless of topic.

Domain names are purchased (although leased would be a more accurate term) from a domain registrar. These registrars are companies such as www.godaddy.com who are authorized by ICANN (Internet Corporation for Assigned Names and Numbers, the international organization that assigns internet names) to sell these names. Most web hosting companies either are registrars or partner with registrars to provide name registration services.

Web hosting companies are companies that provide the computers, internet connection, and services to put your website on the internet.

The TLD (Top Level Domain) is the portion of the name on the end, for example .com, .net or .org. There are a lot more of them today but those three still represent the three largest groups for typical users. There are also .gov, .edu and country codes such as .us for the United States and .ca for Canada.

Using the correct TLD means that there are fairly clearly defined uses for most of the TLDs you see today. .com is for a commercial business, .net is a network (think internet service provider, health care network, etc.), and .org is for organizations such as clubs.

Can you use a .net instead of a .com? Sure! Some people will never know the difference. Those who are tech savvy however may look down on your business for using the wrong TLD. Should you care? That depends, how much business are you willing to lose because you use the incorrect TLD? Personally I would prefer to have every customer I can get, losing one is one too many.

Another factor to consider is that for savvy computer users on Windows machines you can open a browser and type "allans-stuff" without the quotes into the address bar and then press your Ctrl+Enter keys to have the browser automatically add the "www." In the front and ".com" in the back completing the address www.allans-stuff.com and loading the webpage automatically. Shift+Enter does the same for .net and Ctrl+Shift+Enter works for .org. Other TLDs do not have such keyboard shortcuts.

There are tons more TLDs than the few I mention and you can see a complete list at https://en.wikipedia.org/wiki/List_of_Internet_top-level_domains.

The next portion of a domain name is the Second-Level Domain or SLD. This is the Yahoo portion of the Yahoo.com domain name and is what you are primarily concerned with choosing.

When selecting a domain name shorter is always better and clearer is always better. Let's look at these statements one at a time.

www.ibm.com is a great domain name, www.internationalbusinessmachines.com would be appropriate but a lot harder to type. While it is not likely you will get a three letter domain name with a .com TLD you should still understand the easier it is for your customer to type in the name, the more likely it is they will do so.

Keeping the names clear is a difficult thing to do. You want the name to be obvious, uncluttered and to the point. If the domain name confuses people then they will be less likely to remember it. I picked www.paperbirdtek.com because my logo was an origami bird, one that I could and very frequently did make for the customer. When they thought of me, my logo or the origami bird it all came back to the paper bird and since I was a computer technician I thought the tek on the end would add a little quirk to it.

There are lots of things that may or may not work but always try to make it easy for your clients to remember and easy for they to type. Using numbers for letters may make you think you are cool, but it will not make your clients think the same unless you are looking for respect from the extremely young.

When picking a domain name you may also want to consider an Exact Match Domain (or EMD). These are typically difficult to get and there is some debate as to whether they are of any benefit to you in where you appear in search results. Regardless of other possible benefits they do indeed make it easier for your customer to remember you.

EMDs are usually one word or a short phrase that would be exactly what a person would search for in a search engine with no symbols or numbers (unless the number would normally be included in the customer's search terms). An example might be if they were looking for kites then kites.com would be an EMD. EMDs that short are all but impossible to find but you might find slightly longer permutations such as stuntkites.com or howtoflystuntkites.com both of which are good EMDs.

EMDs might be excellent for helping a customer find you but you will have to balance that with having a unique brand identity and other factors to ultimately decide what you want in a domain name.

You should also avoid names that have other company or trademarked names in it. Names such as ImprovedIphone.com and CheaperThanAmazon.net might sound like a good idea but they are likely to get you a letter from a lawyer.

One last thing to remember when picking a domain name is to have other people look at it to see what you may have missed. A domain name may look different to different people. Examples include:

KidsExchange.net   KidSexChange.net

PartnersTalking.com   PartnerStalking.com

LoveTherapist.com   LoveTheRapist.com

To register a domain name, I would suggest you try to do it through your web host as this makes things much faster and easier.

The next part is the web host. This is the company that actually takes your data and makes it available online for other people to find. The domain registrar and web host could be the same people and they typically are, however they can be different as well.

Each web host will have packages available for you to choose from. These packages will provide different things for different prices. We will discuss this in more detail later as we talk about selecting a WordPress friendly web host.

Website files are all of the documents, images, videos and even sounds that make a website work. It includes a lot of files that the visitor may not even see as they control how things are laid out.

A typical old style website would contain a file named index.html which was the first page displayed to the visitor when they went to your website. That file would include information on the color of the background, the font the text should be in (including size, face, bold/underline/italic, color, justification, etc.), links to images that should be displayed (including size and other parameters) and of course the text itself.

Any links that appeared on the web page would cause the browser to open a new web page with another name, such as aboutus.html.

As the web grew and became more interactive, websites started including programming languages such as PHP and Java into the mix to allow things to move and react to visitor input. This also allows for web applications which is how you can enter values on a website and click a button to get a result. For example when you go to a weather website and enter your zip code to get the weather forecast for your area. The moving weather radar you see on that site is another example of a web application.

All of the things that make all of this work are the website files.

1.2 What is a web browser?

A web browser is a program that runs on a device (phone, tablet) or computer (desktop or laptop) that displays a web page to the user. Common browsers include Internet Explorer, Firefox and Chrome to name a few.

Browsers are usually included with the operating system on your computer (or device) such as Internet Explorer and Edge coming with Windows computers, Safari coming with Macintosh computers and Chrome coming with Chromebooks.

You can also download browsers such as Firefox and Chrome for most operating systems out there (Windows, MacOS and Linux).

These programs take code (HTML, PHP, and Java) and present it to the user in the way the author of the website intended.

Code such as this:

```
<HTML>
Hello World!</ br>
It's me!
</HTML>
```

Would display this:

Hello Word!
It's me!

The idea was to make code that could be displayed in any browser (Firefox, Internet Explorer, Chrome) on any platform (phone, tablet, computer although back when the web was created smartphones and tablets really didn't exist) with any operating system (Windows, MacOS, Linux) and the user experience would be the same.

Unfortunately that is rarely the case. There are often minor differences in not only the way a page is displayed to the user, but also in the way it reacts to input from the user. This makes life pretty hard on the website developers.

WordPress is an open source project meaning that tons of people from all over the world work on it. The big advantage here is that those people test it in whatever browser they like to use. This means that it is often better tested on a wider array of browsers, platforms and operating systems than many commercial products or websites.

This is fantastic because it means that you are less likely to run into problems with your websites and certain users not being able to use your website because it won't work right with a specific browser on a specific platform.

Note that I said less likely. Unfortunately there is no silver bullet and while most websites will be perfectly acceptable on virtually any browser/platform/OS combination there are a few things to think about.

Every single Windows computer shipped in the last decade has included Internet Explorer and the majority of end users do not change that. Every single Macintosh shipped in the past decade has come with Safari and the majority of users do not change that either.

What this means is that if you need your website to be as compatible as possible then be sure you check it with these two browsers first.

The odds are that anyone reading this book will have no problems with their website displaying on any modern device or computer but it never hurts to check and make sure. I personally have had a problem with a plugin that was supposed to make the website faster by caching certain items. That plugin had a problem with certain browsers including the one I used most of the time, so I wasted no time in uninstalling it.

Better to check and make sure than have users who can't use your site correctly.

1.3 The difference between an app and an application

There is a lot of confusion on this issue as the lines have been blurred between them and most people I know use the terms pretty much interchangeably. What follows are the definitions as far as this book is concerned. We need to standardize on one definition so that you know what I mean when I say app versus application as they are different to me.

An application is a computer program written for a desktop or laptop operating system. I specified the operating system because you have tablets such as the Microsoft Surface that even though they are indeed tablets they run an operating system and programs (or applications) that are identical to a desktop or laptop computer.

You can install any application on a Surface that you could on a desktop computer with equal or greater system specifications (amount of hard drive space, memory and CPU speed).

Application do not require a network or internet connection to run. They may need that connection to install or activate but not to actually run. Examples include Microsoft Office, QuickBooks and Adobe Photoshop.

Apps are smaller and generally run on devices (smartphones, tablets, etc.). There are apps for full computers (Windows and Macintosh for example) which are pretty much programs that display web data in a local program window.

A good example of an app for Windows would be the Facebook app. You can open a web browser and go to www.facebook.com to use your Facebook account or you can open the Windows Store on your Windows computer and download the Facebook app to do the same thing. Think of the Facebook app as another web browser that only goes to one website, Facebook, and is customized to display that site very well.

1.4 What is WordPress?

WordPress is an open source program that serves up web pages and associated content. It allows the creator (or admin from this point on) to work by pointing, clicking and typing instead of writing code to make the website work.

Technically WordPress is a Content Management System (CMS). It manages the content you provide. This content can be text, images, videos, audio clips, PDFs and more. There are many other CMS programs out there including Joomla and Drupal. Of these, WordPress is currently the most popular.

Open source means that the source code for the software (the programming code that makes it work) is freely available for download from WordPress.org. Downloading the source code allows you to see exactly how it works, change the code to suit your taste (assuming you are a programmer) and you can even contribute to the WordPress project and have your code included in the product.

WordPress is scalable meaning it is equally adept at providing a single page website as it is at providing a website with thousands of pages, thousands of images, hundreds of videos, a complete forum and much more.

In the past each page was a static object, much like a page of a book. In order to change it you opened that page, edited the content and then uploaded that changed page to your web host. Often these changes required specialized software be installed on the computer you wished to edit the page on such as Microsoft's Expression Web or Adobe's Contribute.

WordPress changes this by allowing you to log into the control panel from any computer with an internet connection and web browser such as Internet Explorer, Firefox or Chrome and edit content, change design attributes and upload new media right there. No more need for Expression Web or Contribute.

In addition, WordPress allows multiple people from all over the world to work on one website at the same time. Users can contribute content in a variety of ways with security protocols in place to make sure only the users you want to be able to do a particular task can.

WordPress works with what are called themes. These are the basic design layouts and color schemes of the website and can be changed in seconds. Granted not everything works well with every theme but a lot of the time if you need to change the entire theme, or even one element of a theme such as a font style, you can do it in one place and it will make the changes to all the web pages instantly. Previously changing the font in all your pages could take weeks or longer for large sites.

Now you are probably wondering if it makes all this possible (and a lot more) it must be pretty expensive, right? Actually no, it is completely free. Not just free for personal use, but free for business use as well.

1.5 WordPress.com vs WordPress.org

Many people have a hard time with the difference between these two so I wanted to take a minute to explain this.

WordPress.org is the website devoted to the development, discussion, and support of the free open source WordPress program.

WordPress.com is a website devoted to providing both free and paid web hosting services specifically designed for people wanting to use WordPress from WordPress.org.

WordPress.com would not exist without the program from WordPress.org however WordPress.org would not have a problem without WordPress.com.

Although many WordPress.com staff regularly contribute to the code base of WordPress and even though there are some of the same people at both places, the two sites are not related in any legal or technical way.

Section 2: Getting WordPress running

Previously when designing a website you purchased software like Microsoft's Expression Web or Adobe's Contribute and installed that on your personal computer. You used those programs to edit files one at a time on your computer and uploaded them to a server once each file was complete.

In addition to these files you had all your media such as images, PDFs, and videos that had to be organized into folders (hopefully) and uploaded as well.

Instead of that we now need to install the WordPress program on your website and let it do most of the heavy lifting. We don't need specialized software installed on our computer to edit the website and in fact, we can edit the website from any computer with an internet connection and a web browser from anywhere in the world.

We still have the same media files including images, PDFs, and videos but we no longer have to deal with HTML, PHP, and CSS files that could number in the hundreds.

In order to do that, you first need to have a domain name and hosting service (either paid or a free one from WordPress.com). We talked a little about that and now we will discuss finding a WordPress friendly service (or getting a free one from WordPress.com) in much more detail.

2.1 Selecting a WordPress friendly hosting service

Let's start by discussing some terms we will need to know before selecting a service.

Shared hosting means you, and several other people, are all sharing one computer and one connection for hosting your sites. This is usually fine for smaller sites and even some medium sites. Shared is definitely the cheapest type of plan. This would be an excellent place to start.

Non-shared, dedicated hosting, etc. type of plans usually mean you have your own machine, or virtual machine, and your own connection (or virtual connection) to the internet. This is always faster and always more expensive. If you are on a shared plan and start to notice that your page load times (how long it takes for someone to click on a link in your website and then for the page to completely load) become excessively long, you might need to switch over to one of these.

There can be different levels of these "more dedicated" plans that range from double the price of a shared plan to over a thousand dollars a month for a powerful machine that does nothing but host your one website.

Managed plans usually refer to managing your WordPress installation. This means they keep things up to date, worry about PHP version compatibility and things like that. Most of this you can do yourself with a minimum of time and effort and most of it I will walk you through (like keeping updates done automatically with a plugin, more on that later).

Where managed plans really shine is you are completely new to this and not really a do-it-yourselfer is that they often offer 24/7 WordPress technical support. This doesn't usually mean they support all your themes and plugins but it does mean that if you have a problem with WordPress itself, they can help.

Truth be told most web hosting services are pretty WordPress friendly these days. Most of the websites I have worked on were on www.hostrocket.com and www.1and1.com. Neither of these are really WordPress centric or specialist hosts however they both work well. In fact I personally have five WordPress installations of my own on 1and1 and that was the host for the examples in this book.

The reason for my using these services is that most of my customers and I are all coming from having an existing website and migrated over to WordPress. Since we didn't want to switch hosts unless we had to, we kept on rolling with who we had and have had virtually no problems.

To state this another way, if you have an existing web host there is probably no reason to switch unless you are pretty sure you need a feature such as WordPress technical support that your current host does not offer.

There is however no doubt that certain hosts which are specialized towards WordPress can offer a simpler and better experience in many cases for the novice. If nothing else they may have some technical support personnel who are experienced with WordPress and can help you if you run into problems integrating your installation with their servers.

You can see the most current list of WordPress recommend hosting services at https://WordPress.org/hosting/ but we can certainly cover a couple right here.

DreamHost (www.dreamhost.com) is a California based hosting company that has for many years been a favorite of WordPress users. Plans here start at $7.95 a month for a managed, shared hosting service. If you outgrow that plan they can bump you up to their DreamPress plan which is much faster and scales better as you get more users for only $16.95 a month.

Both of these plans require you to either have your own domain name or pay for a domain name from them which runs $13.95 a year for a .com TLD for the first year. They do offer some sales so your first year could be cheaper for less popular TLDs such as .club, .xyz or .site.

BlueHost (www.bluehost.com) in Utah is another favorite in the WordPress community and offers plans for managed WordPress hosting starting at $19.99 per month (currently on sale). While more expensive than some others, their packages offer an included domain name, static IP address and a control panel based on the widely used and very popular cPanel which usually is an additional charge.

BlueHost to me is more a place to use for a medium sized business or someone who needs all the expandability and flexibility you can get in a managed solution. It is also a good place to go for non-managed plans which start at $2.75 a month (again, on sale right now, down from $7.99) which includes a domain name (for the first year. If you cancel early, you have to pay for the domain name).

While their extremely inexpensive account is cheap, it also puts pretty serious restrictions on the number of email accounts you can have and the amount of email you can store in them. It still may be a good choice for a person looking to put up a low traffic personal account who doesn't need much. Besides you can always upgrade to a higher end plan.

Oddly enough, missing from the recommended WordPress hosting list is one that I see mentioned all the time in other places and in other books, www.WordPress.com.

WordPress.com has plans ranging from free to just under $25 a month depending on what you want or need. The free account is great for someone who just wants to get their personal blog online or share information with friends and family. Be aware however that the free package does not allow you to use your own domain name (you will get a subdomain of WordPress.com such as yourname.WordPress.com) and they will put advertising on your website which you have no control over.

Since the hosting is free and they do offer a lot in exchange for the little bit of advertising it is still a pretty good deal.

Moving up to the $2.99 a month package gets you your own domain name included in the price, email and live chat support, and removal of all the ads.

The big draw to WordPress.com of course is the free accounts and we will be looking at those later in the book.

If you want to stick with your existing host or want to use a host that we have not talked about, a simple email or phone call to their sales or technical support department should provide you with any answers you need about WordPress support.

2.2 Use your web host's installer or do it yourself?

There are two different methods of installation and both have good and bad points.

Your web host may have an installer that runs with a single click of a mouse (OK, maybe a little more than a single click) on their control panel. This can be very attractive as it is by far the easiest way to install it and almost always guarantees compatibility with your web host and all their software.

Virtually all major web hosts have this feature, and even many of the little guys. If in doubt, just ask, they all know what you are talking about when you ask if they have a "WordPress installer in their control panel".

The down side of doing it this way is that they don't always have the latest version, don't always keep their versions up to date, and are not always compatible with the latest plugins you may want to use. In fact, some of them might even restrict what plugins and themes you can use (although this is rare).

Even though using your host's installer is the fastest and easiest method, it is also the option I recommend the least simply because you often give up some of your control.

The second option is to install WordPress from scratch on your web host and although it is more time consuming and harder, it is by no means overly difficult. This method ensures you are running the most current version of WordPress which is important because it patches any security vulnerabilities and errors that they have found since they released the previous version. Just like in Windows, MacOS and Linux it is important to keep up to date.

This method also makes sure you can run any theme or plugin you choose.

I like control (ask my wife, or for that matter, my boss!)

2.2.1 Using your web host's installer

Every host is probably completely different so I can only show you an example to give you an idea. Use this as more a guideline of general things you can expect; not as a step by step guide.

If 1and1 is your web host here is the basic procedure. Keep in mind that these procedures change from time to time and should be used only as a guideline. They were correct as of the date I grabbed the screenshots and probably different the next day:

Go to www.1and1.com and log into your control panel.

Under the Hosting section you will see a selection named WordPress, click there.

Give your website a name and click the blue Create Website button.

Here you can create an account to be the administrator. Do not use the name "admin" or "administrator" as these will be the first things someone will guess when trying to hack your site. Enter your password twice, check the box agreeing to give up your first born and then click the blue Continue button.

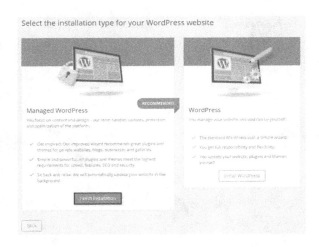

Here you have a choice of letting them mostly manage it or for you to do it yourself. I typically like to do it myself rather than wait on them to apply security updates and the second option allows for a wider array of plugins as well.

Clicking on the first option presents you with the screen above. You can then click on the blue Edit Website button to log into your WordPress installation.

Typically after the installation you can also log in to your WordPress administration screen by going to www.yourdomain.com/wp-admin/.

2.2.2 Installing WordPress from scratch

The first thing you need to do for a full installation is download the WordPress package from www.WordPress.org using the blue button which is normally near the middle of the screen and says something like "Download WordPress 4.6.1" where 4.6.1 is the most current version number they have for release.

Once it is in your download folder you can extract the zip file (or the tar.gz if you downloaded that version and are on Linux). For Windows users you can simply right click on the file and select Extract All.

Now open your file explorer and browse to the directory where you extracted the files. In my case that was c:\users\allan\downloads\WordPress-4.6.1

In this directory you should see a another directory named WordPress, open that and inside is a file named wp-config-sample.php. Rename that file to wp-config.php. You can now right click on that file and select Open With and then find and select Notepad.

Once loaded in notepad you should see the following:

```
// ** MySQL settings - You can get this info from your web host ** //
/** The name of the database for WordPress */
define('DB_NAME', 'database_name_here');

/** MySQL database username */
define('DB_USER', 'username_here');

/** MySQL database password */
define('DB_PASSWORD', 'password_here');

/** MySQL hostname */
define('DB_HOST', 'localhost');
```

In that configuration file there are four things you need to find out so you can change them; database name, user name, password and host name. With 1and1 those items look like db123456789 for database name, dbo123456789 for user name, whatever password you give the database and db123456789.1and1.com.

With 1and1 you can not change the database names but with other providers you may be able to. For security, do not use WP or DB as the prefix (beginning) of a WordPress database name.

Let's walk through the 1and1 database setup so you have an idea what all this means.

From the main 1and1 control panel you need to scroll down until you see MySQL Database under Manage Webspace.

Click on the MySQL Database link to see the database page.

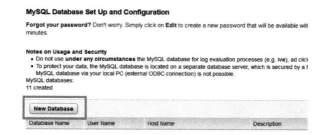

Now click on the New Database button.

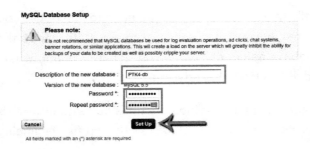

Here you enter a name for the database and the password twice. I am working with the domain name PTK4.com so I used ptk4-db as my database name. This helps me keep track of which database is for what. Now click the blue button labeled Set Up.

This screen shows you all the rest of the information we needed. Write all this down, take a screen capture or print it out and be sure you put the password you created with it.

Switch back to the configuration file we opened in notepad and let's put in our information:

// ** MySQL settings - You can get this info from your web host ** //
/** The name of the database for WordPress */
define('DB_NAME', db123456789);

/** MySQL database username */
define('DB_USER', dbo123456789);

/** MySQL database password */
define('DB_PASSWORD', Pass!wrd123);

26

db123456789.db.1and1.com

Save the configuration file by selecting File and Save from the notepad menu. Now we can close notepad.

Next we need an FTP program to upload our WordPress installation and the one I prefer is FileZilla (www.filezilla-project.org). Download the client version from their website and install it.

Now on your 1and1 control panel you can select Secure FTP Account under Manage Webspace.

On the screen that follows look for the first ftp account username, we will need this later.

This number will be different for each account so make sure you write this down correctly and not share it with anyone.

Now launch FileZilla.

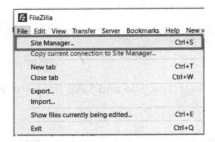

Select File and then Site Manager.

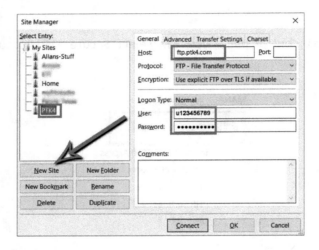

Click on the New Site button over on the lower left side, enter a name on the upper left pane, then put in ftp.yourdomain.com on the top right and then the username we got from the sftp portion of the 1and1 control panel and finally the password for your 1and1 account (the same one you use to log into your 1and1 control panel in most cases).

I used ftp.ptk4.com because I am working with my domain name of ptk4.com. Yours will be whatever you bought from the registrar which may have been 1and1 or someone else. In my case here, it was 1and1 I bought ptk4.com from.

Now click the Connect button on the bottom center.

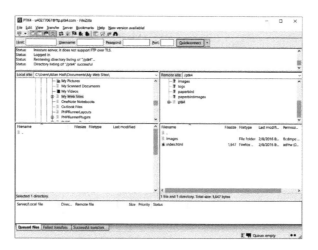

Once connected you will see the screen above, or a rough approximation. This screen is divided into two sides; the left is the local side and displays files and folders on your computer, the right is the remote side and displays files and folders on the web site. You may notice that I already have an images folder and a single file on the right side of mine.

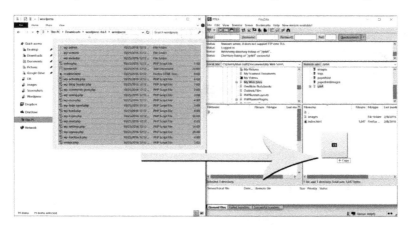

With the folder open where you extracted all the WordPress files and also where you renamed and edited the wp-config.php file (in my case c:\users\allan\downloads\WordPress-4.6.1\WordPress), highlight all the files and folders in that directory and then click and drag them all over to the right pane and then release the mouse. This will transfer all the files and folders from your computer to your website.

Once you are done your right side should look similar to this:

What you should not see is a WordPress directory. If you see only a WordPress directory you need to delete that off the server (the right side), open the WordPress folder on the left side and copy the **contents** of the WordPress folder on the left to the folder on the right so you see something like what is shown in the previous image.

You can now close Filezilla, open a web browser and go to www.yourdomain.com/wp-admin/ to see your administration screen: (this is also how you will log into the administration screen from now on)

Here you need to select your language (probably English if you are reading this book) and click the blue Continue button in the bottom right.

On this screen you will need to enter the name of your website, a username for your account (do not use admin or administrator as these are the first ones hackers guess), a secure password and then a valid email address. If you use what WordPress thinks is a weak password it will require you to check a box to confirm that you want to use a weak password.

Finally click the Install WordPress button in the bottom right.

This next screen just shows the status as successful and your chosen username, click Log In at the bottom.

Enter your chosen username and password and then click the blue Log In button on the bottom right.

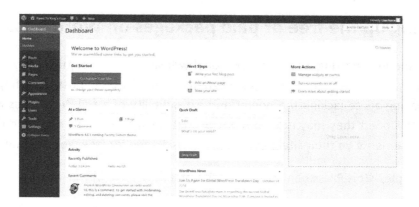

Congratulations! You have completed the installation of WordPress and are at the administration screen for your brand new website.

After the installation you can log in to your WordPress administration screen by going to www.yourdomain.com/wp-admin/.

2.3 Setting up the free or paid packages on WordPress.com

A lot of people just starting out with a personal website or one for their very small home based business may want something as inexpensive and easy as possible. They may also not mind having a site lacking the power and extendibility of a full WordPress installation because at this point they may not need any of that. Lastly, they may not mind if there are a few advertisements on their site placed there in exchange for free web hosting.

For these people, WordPress.com has your solution in the form of free hosting.

Let's set up a website from scratch on WordPress.com and see how it goes. This will let you see if this is for you. If you are sure this is where you want to start you can follow along in your web browser and create your own account as I create mine or you can just read along and see what is here before you jump in.

To start with, let's point our browser to www.WordPress.com and take a look at their home page.

One thing that WordPress.com excels at is making things easy. Right here on their home page all we need to do is click the blue button that says Create Website. That takes us to a page where we can start telling them a little about what we want to do.

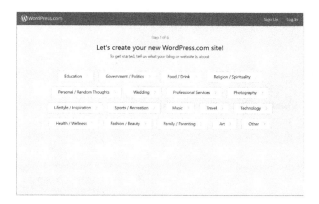

On this page we can select a category for our new website. In this example I am going to create a website about stunt kites so I will select Sports/Recreation from the list.

The next screen we see shows us several different layouts for the website. The first is what we would expect for a standard blog which is what I want, the second is a static introduction page, the third is a grid which would be good for a photography website and the last would be excellent for an online shopping website.

I am going to click on the top left design.

The next screen allows us to pick a theme from nine different selections. Remember that themes can be modified so how it looks here does not have to be exactly the way it stays. You can also skip this step by clicking the link at the bottom that says skip for now.

I am going to select Penscratch as one to start with which then takes us to the domain selection screen:

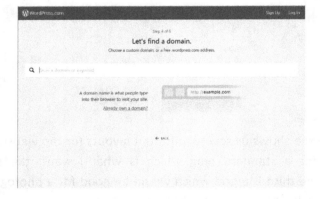

Once you start typing a domain name into the box a list will be shown below to help you find a selection. This list will include not only paid domain names but also free ones as shown in the next image.

It took me a few minutes and a bunch of tries to get a free domain name at the top that I liked. Once I found one I simply clicked the blue Select button over on the right of that name and that took me to the screen to pick a plan:

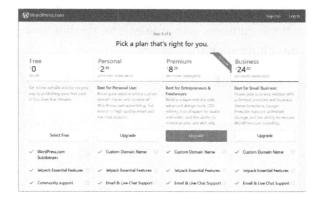

Since I want to start out as inexpensively as possible I am going to select the free plan on the left by clicking the Select Free button on the left side about half way down the page. You could of course pick a paid plan here with more options however that does not change the signup process.

Enter your email address in the top field and if you want, you can change the username in the second field. In the bottom box enter a strong password, one that consists of both upper and lower case letters, numbers and at least one symbol. Once you do that click the big blue Create My Account button on the bottom.

The next screen informs you that they sent an email to your email address to confirm your account. Check your email and you should find one similar to this:

Clicking the blue Confirm Now box in the middle takes you to a WordPress.com login page.

Enter the username and password you selected earlier and that should log you in to your new WordPress website.

That's it, you have a brand new WordPress website set up and hosted for free. Time to start adding content!

After the installation you can log in to your WordPress administration screen by going to www.yourdomain.com/wp-admin/ (gets you the full administration screen) or by visiting www.WordPress.com and clicking on the Log In button in the upper right (gets you the streamlined administration screen).

Section 3: Using WordPress

Installing WordPress was fun and you should feel a sense of accomplishment because that was the single most difficult task when dealing with WordPress. If you made it this far, you can relax knowing everything from here on out is a little easier.

Now we move from getting it running to actually making it usable. This is where we learn how WordPress works and how to bend it to our will in our quest for internet domination. If you think I am sitting here petting my dog "Mini Me" while uttering that last sentence you would be wrong, she is a cat whose name is Bebay (bee bay) and she is so spoiled she has her own mini me.

WordPress is an extremely flexible platform and as such it has a lot to offer but we first have to learn all the terminology and where to find everything. That is where this section starts.

Here we go through the entire administration area of our WordPress installation and look at virtually every single option and screen. I don't expect you to remember it all, but going through it all like this tends to help me remember things. "I remember there was some setting for changing that somewhere, now where was that?" Then I can look it up in the index, glossary, or by re-reading the section in question.

A little later in the book we will get to what order to do what in so for right now just open up your web browser and follow along!

3.1 Full WordPress installations

Using and managing WordPress requires that we understand and be able to use the administration screen. This is a series of screens and menus that allows us to configure, add to, and manage our WordPress website. That is what this section will teach you.

There are several ways to install and use WordPress however if you know how to use the full installation the rest will be considerably easier as anything other than the full installations are just more streamlined versions of the same thing.

In fact, if you use WordPress.com as your host you can log in two different ways to get two different interfaces for WordPress. Not to worry, one is the full installation and one is their streamlined version based off the full installation.

Even if you never intend on using the full version of WordPress I highly recommend you read this entire section as it will teach you everything you need to get started using the program.

One interesting note is that if you learn to use the full version right up front, then you can reasonably expect to be able to use (maybe with just a little figuring things out) any WordPress installation on any platform or host out there. Neat eh?

In addition, I refer back to this section assuming you have read it in later sections.

Anyway, let's get rolling!

3.1.1 The administration screen

To get to your administration screen you need to go to www.yourdomain.com/wp-admin/ and enter your username and password.

The administration screen is divided into two sides; the left which is the navigation menu side or sidebar and the right which is the work area and in this case is displaying the dashboard. When you select a menu on the left side options are presented on the right side. Virtually everything you need to do in WordPress starts with this layout idea; select the menu on the left, work with that menu on the right.

In addition to the two sides there is also a toolbar across the top.

Both the menu and dashboard are dynamic meaning that they change as things change. For example when you add a plugin (discussed later) that plugin might create a new menu item over on the left. Selecting that new menu item on the left could present configuration options over on the right related to that plugin.

On the dashboard the top section can be dismissed by clicking on the little X in the top right corner of the Welcome to WordPress! Area and I usually do that immediately as there is nothing in that section I cannot get to with the menus.

Next down on the left side of the dashboard you see boxes like At a Glance and Activity in which the contents will change as you add more pages and posts (more on those later). By default there are two other boxes; one for Quick Draft so you can jot down ideas in a hurry and another for WordPress News so you can keep up to date on the latest in the WordPress community.

Note on the far right the dashed line box that says Drag Boxes Here. This should be a clue to the configurability of the dashboard in that you can drag the boxes around, remove them or even add new ones. You may have also noticed that each little box has a triangle in its upper right corner which allows you to collapse that box so that only the title shows.

You can further configure the dashboard (and many other areas of the administration screens) by clicking near the upper right where you see Screen Options tab with the little downward pointing triangle:

Here we see a series of options with checkboxes next to them. In this example they are all checked meaning they all show up on the dashboard. If I want to remove a box from the dashboard I simply uncheck the box and it disappears. When I am done here I can click the Screen Options tab which now has an upward pointing triangle and the menu goes away.

Now let's move to the upper left under the word Dashboard and talk about the navigation menu.

Home is the same as clicking on the Dashboard above it, this is where it always starts when you log in.

Updates is a central screen to find information about updates for your website. If you have updates available you might see something like the following:

Here you see a circle next to Updates with a number in it indicating how many updates you have available. Clicking on the Updates menu item presents you with the following screen:

Here you are shown what all updates are available, warned to make backups before updating, and allow to perform the updates.

Once all updates are done you should see this screen.

This screen shows you when you last checked for a new version, what version you currently have and that you have no more updates available for WordPress, plugins, or themes. It also gives you the option to reinstall your current version if something goes horribly wrong.

It is always important to keep your system up to date as this patches not only flaws that could cause your website to behave incorrectly but also could allow hackers and viruses into your system.

Some plugins may also show you updates over on the navigation menus (more about plugins in a little while). When this happens you may see something like this:

In this image I have two plugins installed; Yoast SEO and Photo Gallery. Both of them currently are showing notifications in the little circles with the number one in them over on the navigation menu.

This notification can mean an update or it could mean something else but if you click on the menu item with the number out beside it, it will tell you what is going on. Just be aware that some plugins show you their need for being updated in this way.

3.1.1.1 Posts

The next item down on the menu is posts. You may notice that if you hover your mouse over the word Posts on the left a little fly-out menu will appear. If you click on the word Posts on the right side of the screen, or work area, where the dashboard was is now the posts screen and those items you saw on the fly-out menu are now listed under the word Posts on the left menu. I call those items the sub-menu.

On the Posts screen a list of all the current posts appears on the right with some information including Title, Author, Categories, Tags and more. You can also see options for Bulk Actions, filtering by dates and categories and a button for Add New. You can edit a post by clicking on its title.

Looking in the upper right we see the Screen Options tab which when clicked shows us the following:

Here we can change some of the things that appear on the screen as well as how many posts are displayed per screen before it makes a second page and so on. While I normally leave these as default it is important to note that as you add plugins they can add things to the display which you may or may not want shown. The image above is of a default installation of WordPress while the following image is after installing the Yoast SEO plugin we will talk about later.

Columns

☑ Author ☑ Categories ☑ Tags ☑ Comments ☑ Date ☑ SEO ☑ Readability ☐ SEO Title ☐ Meta Desc. ☐ Focus KW

Pagination

Number of items per page: 20

View Mode

⦿ List View   ◯ Excerpt View

Apply

Screen Options ▲

Note how in this second image of the screen options we have several new items including SEO and Readability which are checked and SEO Title, Meta Desc. And Focus KW which are not checked. It is always a good idea to look at your screen options after installing a plugin that might add columns or features to your pages like this.

Let's take a look at the display All (1) | Published (1). This allows you to view all your posts or just the ones that have been published. The number inside the parenthesis is the number of articles of that type. In this example there is only one post and it is published so the numbers are the same. If you create a new post and save it as a draft you might see something similar to this All (2) | Published (1) | Draft (1).

Next is the Bulk Actions dropdown box. This allows you to select multiple posts (by clicking in the little checkbox next to the post title, or the very top checkbox which selects all the posts) and then select an action in the dropdown box (either Edit or Move to Trash) and then click the Apply box to the right of the Bulk Action dropdown box to execute the action.

If you send one to the trash using the bulk actions or the little menu that displays when you hover over a post's title, that moves it to the trash much like Windows moves files into the recycle bin, but doesn't actually delete the file. Once you send one to the trash you will see the display we were just looking at to something like All (1) | Published (1) | Trash (1). Items in the trash are not counted in the All or any other section. Clicking in the Trash (1) link changes our list to show only those items in the trash and hovering the mouse over the post's title shows the following options:

☐ **My First Post**
Restore | Delete Permanently

Here you can restore the item (move it out of the trash and put it back exactly as it was before you trashed it) or delete the post permanently. Once deleted, you can no longer get it back.

One thing to note here is that if you delete a post, any comments that may be associated with that post are also deleted. If you trash a post, and later restore it, those comments will be restored as well.

Back on the main Post listing screen to the right of the Bulk Action dropdown box and its associated Apply button is the All Dates and All Categories dropdown boxes with their associated Filter button. The All Dates dropdown will list all the month/year combinations that have posts associated with them so in my example it would only show October 2016. Selecting this and then clicking the Filter button would filter the list to only show posts from October 2016. The All Categories dropdown works the same way but displays a list of all the categories you have created. By default there is only one named Uncategorized. As you create new categories they will automatically appear here.

Later we will discuss the difference between categories and tags but here is a difference right here, there is no way to show only posts with a specific tag on this screen meaning that categories have an important use behind the scenes as well as for the visitor.

Over on the right side at about this level you see an empty text box with a button to the right that says Search Posts. If you enter something into the box and click the button the system will filter the results shown in the list to include only those posts that include the search term in any place in the post. This will search the title as well as the actual text of the post.

A good example you can try right now is to type the word "delete" in the box (without the quotes of course) and click the Search Posts button. Notice that the results are the same because you only have one post and that post does contain the word delete, just not in the title. If you click the title of the post and read the post once it opens you will see the word is indeed in the text of the post.

Back at our main Posts screen we have the list we have already talked some about which includes the title, author, category, tags, number of comments and finally the date it was published.

The title is pretty obvious but author has something interesting to note. The name that is displayed defaults to the name you used to log in, in this example, admin. We can change that. Click up at the very top right where you see Howdy, admin (or whatever name you choose as the administrator since I told you not to use admin or administrator). Now click Edit My Profile.

Scroll down a little ways in your profile to find this:

Now type in a First Name, Last Name and a Nickname. Now use the dropdown box labeled Display name publicly as to select one of several options based on your information including the original admin name, your first name, your last name, your first name comma last name, etc.

Now scroll down to the bottom of the page and click the blue button labeled Update Profile. Once you do, your new chosen name will appear in the top right where it says Howdy, Your Name. Clicking on the Posts menu option on the left to go back to the Posts main page will now display Your Name as the author instead of admin (or whatever you picked).

Continuing on with our discussion of the posts listing the next items over after author are categories and tags which should be pretty obvious now. The next one is just a little icon that looks like one of those boxes you read in cartoons to see what people are saying, and that isn't too far from the truth. This column will show you how many comments have been submitted to this post. More on comments later.

Lastly we have date which of course is obvious.

If you hover your mouse over the names of these columns you might notice that some of them, Title, Comments and Dates to be specific, have a triangle that appears to the right. These triangles allow you to sort the list based on those columns. For example you could click the one next to date to sort the list in date descending order (when the triangle points down) and click it again to sort them by date ascending order (when the triangle points up).

You can also hover the mouse over the title of the post and see a little menu appear below the title.

Clicking edit gets you the same thing as clicking on the title of the post while Quick Edit gets you a nifty little editor and allows you to change some of the fundamental aspects of the post, such as this:

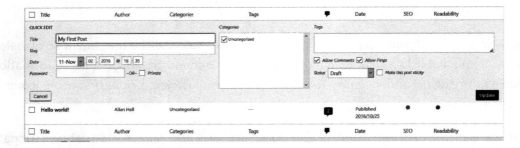

With this screen you can change the title, slug (simply the title of the post with the spaces turned into dashes and stripped of punctuation, this makes it usable in a web address where you cannot have spaces or punctuation), date and a variety of other options of the post. One important note is the section over near the center on the right side; Allow Comments. This is how you can turn on and off comments for an individual post.

After Quick Edit you see Trash which deletes the post and Preview which of course shows you a preview of the post.

On the bottom of the post list you will see another Bulk Actions and Apply button so you can work from the bottom of a long list without having to scroll all the way back to the top and a total number of posts over on the right.

This completes our discussion of the main Posts page so let's move over to the sub-menu over on the left.

Remember when we first looked at the menu you could move your mouse over the word Posts and it showed a fly-out menu. Once we clicked on the word Posts however the fly-out disappeared and those options moved underneath the word Posts to become a sub-menu.

This sub-menu has four options; All Posts (which is where we are already, the same as clicking on the word Posts), Add New (which is the same thing we already did, click Posts and then the Add New button at the top), Categories and Tags which allow us to manage categories and tags respectively. We will get into Categories and Tags in some detail in a few minutes.

If you are logged into your WordPress administration screen and go view your website you will see a few things are a little different. One such example is the following:

Note the arrow is pointing to a link called Edit. Clicking on this link takes you into the standard post edit screen we will soon be talking about. This is a great way to spend some time reading your website, find an error, edit and correct it, then continue on reading your site.

3.1.1.1.1 Add New

Let's create a new post so we can understand what some of this is, go ahead and click on the Add New button at the top of the Posts screen.

The Add New Post screen appears and it looks a lot like a simplified word processor. This makes sense because creating web pages is about presenting information to the visitor and that generally involves a great deal of text.

Again there is our old friend the Screen Options tab which gives us the following options:

This is the first time we have seen default options on the Screen Options box turned off. Each of those options without checkmarks in them will put something else on the screen if we check them, for example the first one without a check in it, Excerpt. Check that box and scroll down to the bottom of the screen and there will be a new section called Excerpt.

Here is where you can type in an excerpt, or a basic description, of what the post is about that some themes will use when providing links to the post in search results, tag, and category archives, etc. They are also used as the summary in RSS feeds (more on those later).

This is hidden by default because if you have not manually put in an excerpt, WordPress will automatically use the first 55 words of the post as the excerpt. This makes things a lot easier but you have to decide if you would prefer WordPress to use the automatic excerpt or if you think you can write a better short description for use as the excerpt.

The next unchecked item is trackbacks and that adds the following box near the bottom of the screen:

In older systems this was where you put the addresses of the systems you want to notify when you link to their posts. The address you put in here would be something like www.allans-stuff.com/trackback/. These are handled mainly by pingbacks now making this only if you need to connect to a legacy system.

Moving to the next unchecked box in our Screen Options menu we see Custom Fields. Clicking that shows us the following section near the bottom of our screen:

This allows us to add extra data, called meta-data, to a post. We can add a field and assign a value to it and have that show up in our post. Examples might include the mood we are in, our current weight, what we had for breakfast, and just about anything else you might want.

After we add a new custom field it will become available from any add or edit post screen so we can just select it from the dropdown box and then enter our value for that post. Each post can use the same custom field(s) but will have only the value you enter for that post.

The down side here is that to make it show up in your post is a little more complex. You can either edit the actual code of your theme or download a plugin to handle it. I recommend you download the Custom Fields Display plugin and use it if you need custom fields.

Don't worry, you will have plenty of experience installing plugins by the end of the book.

Continuing on with our unchecked screen options let's check the Discussion box which shows us this:

Here we can turn on the ability of people to leave comments and whether to allow trackbacks/pingbacks. Generally we will not need to alter these settings however it might be useful to remember where this is in the future. We will discuss comments, trackbacks, and pingbacks a little later.

The last two unchecked items on our screen options are Slug and Author and checking them shows us these boxes near the bottom of the screen:

Here we can change the slug which is generally the title of the text with spaces replaced with dashes and is used in creating a URL directly to the page called a permalink (more on that later).

The author dropdown box allows us to change the author of the post to whoever we like.

When you change a screen option for the posts page it will be changed for all post pages. This means if you put a check in the author checkbox so that the author box is displayed like above, then any time you add or edit a post the box to change the author will be available.

Back at the top of the Add New screen is a box for the title, right below the Add New Post label. Go ahead and put something in there like My First Post and then click in the larger main text area below it. When you do you will notice something appear right below where you typed in your title, the permalink.

Permalink: http://www.ptk4.com/2016/10/25/my-first-post/ Edit

A permalink is a web address directly to this post without having to navigate any menus. This is important in case you want to post a link to this article on another website, in an email or in a press release. You can of course change the permalink by clicking the Edit button right next to it. If you do, note that you can only change the very last part which in this case is the my-first-post portion. If you do change this, do not use any spaces or special characters as it will be very difficult for that to work well when sent through email or typed in.

At the top of the main text box you will see this menu. The button at the top that says Add Media is for exactly that, adding pictures and other files. We will discuss media a little more in depth later on but for now just remember that if you want to add a picture, that is the button you want to press.

You can also simply drag media such as images, audio, and video right into the editor window below the toolbar which is probably how you will do this most of the time.

The default layout for working with your posts is Visual or what we call WYSIWYG (What You See Is What You Get) and that is denoted on the far right with the two tabs labeled Visual and Text. The Text tab allows you to work with the actual HTML code and is probably something you will not do for a very long time.

Just under the Visual/Text tabs is a strange icon that looks like this:

Clicking this enables Distraction Free Writing mode which removes the gray menu down the left side and all the boxes down the right side of the screen while the center area remains the same. The idea here is of course to reduce distractions.

Below all of that is a menu similar to many word processing programs you may have used in the past with a large B for bold, I for italic, the abc for strike through, bullet list, numbered list, blockquote, horizontal line, left justify, center justify, right justify, insert/edit link, remove link, insert read more tag and toggle toolbar.

The insert/edit link icon allows you to place the cursor where you want a link, or highlight a section of text (or image) you want linked, click the link button and type in the URL you want to link to. Here I have highlighted a section of text and clicked the link button:

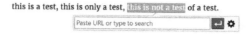

When the link popup appears there is a gear to the right which when clicked displays this window:

From this screen you can edit the URL, change the text that is displayed (what I highlighted), elect to have the link open in a new browser tab, or use the search box to link to existing content on your website.

Once you are done changing options click the blue Add Link button in the bottom right or the Cancel button in the bottom left.

That last option, toggle toolbar, when clicked gives you a second toolbar below the first with more options on it like this:

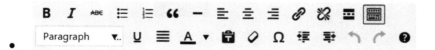

The first drop down box is a style selector, underline, full justify, text color, paste as text, clear formatting, insert special character, decrease indent, increase indent, undo, redo and show keyboard shortcuts.

The dropdown style selector allows you to choose the style of the text such as paragraph, heading 1, heading 2, heading 3, and so on. Headings are extremely important as they help break up the text into organized sections making it easier for visitors to find information. It also makes it easier to read.

The title of a post or page is usually in heading 1 so it is very unadvisable for you to use a heading 1 in your post or page. Try to stick with heading 2 for major areas and heading 3 for more minor areas. Some people however prefer to start with heading 3s like I do. It makes things a little cleaner looking in my opinion.

Most of these should be pretty familiar but if not you can play around with them on a test post to see what happens when you click on them. I promise none of them launch a world ending missile from an underground bunker in the middle of the ocean, meow.

Over on the right you will see a row of boxes all the way down the right side. These are also dynamic in that adding new plugins can add new boxes. We will talk about the default one starting with the top right, where you will see a Publish box. Once you are done working on a post you can go here to save and/or publish it.

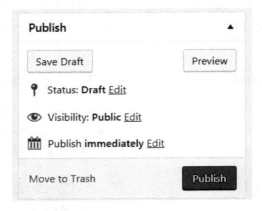

The button on the top that says Save Draft saves the post without publishing it, just like a email draft you may write saves it but does not send it. Preview allows you to see it as a site visitor would see it.

The Status tells you it is a draft and allows you to edit the status. This feature is primarily used in larger sites that have a lot of cooperative writers contributing to the site. By default you can change the status to Pending Review.

The Visibility shows that it is Public, meaning anyone can read it once it is published. Clicking Edit will allow you options including sticking the post to the front page (making a sticky), password protecting the post so that only people with the password can read it or making it private so that only you can read it.

The Publish section shows you that if you click the blue Publish button at the bottom right of this box, it will be published immediately. Clicking on the Edit link allows you to put in a specific time and date for the post to be automatically published. Once you put a date and time in and click the Publish button this will show that it is scheduled and display the date and time. I love this feature so I can write several articles and schedule them and they appear regularly on my website even if I am out of town.

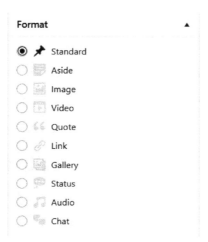

Below the Publish box is the Format box. Certain themes will automatically format pages differently based on these formats. For example a video page may be displayed differently in that theme than a gallery page. Not all themes support this option and not every theme that does support formats support all of them, but it is nice to have the option.

Below the Format box is the Categories box which allows you to assign a category to this post. Categories allow you to break your posts up into smaller chunks where the website visitor can look at only one category. For example, let's say you ran a website about kites and a visitor was only interested in two line stunt kites. You might have categories for many different kite types but the visitor could click on the category box beside your posts and select the one you created just for two line stunt kites. Now they only see posts related to those specific types of kites.

More information on categories is in the next section entitled, Categories.

The next box down is the Tags box and these are another way to aid in navigation by assigning one or more keywords to a post. Tags are typically displayed underneath each post and when a user clicks on one of the tag keywords a page displaying only posts with that keyword is displayed. This works very much like categories however tags are really easy to add keywords to as you write posts instead of having to create a category before populating it.

Once you have been adding tags for a while you can click the link at the bottom of the Tags box that says Choose from the most used tags and select a tag you have already used.

You can read a lot more about tags in a few minutes as there is a section on tags.

The last default box is the Featured Image box. A featured image is a feature that is supported by certain themes where one particular image is specified as the featured image and it is that image that is used in the preview and any thumbnail for the article.

One important thing we have not seen since we started with the Add New button is called revisions. Every time you edit a post or page WordPress makes a new copy of it and keeps the old. If you are editing a post or page and look under the Screen Options you will see an option for revisions.

Easier than that however is that the Publish box over on the right side of the screen will show revisions like this:

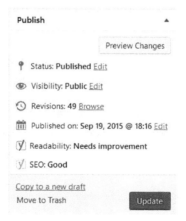

Note that it has added a line that did not used to be there, Revisions. This is followed by the number of revisions and a link labeled Browse. Clicking Browse takes you to this screen:

Here you can hover over any place in the timeline to see the date and time of the revision and then click on the one you want to see two boxes appear at the bottom showing what has been changed.

The box on the left is the old content while the one on the right is the current content. Highlighted portions show what was changed in that one revision.

You can restore a previous revision by using the blue button in the top right labeled Restore This Revision.

Revisions are useful to see if you deleted something you should not have, and for restoring things you didn't mean to do (at least that seems to be how I use them, heh).

Remember that every time you change a post or page WordPress makes a revision you can restore. This includes if you restore a revision. Clicking Restore This Revision will cause WordPress to make a copy of the current page as a revision before restoring the older version.

3.1.1.1.2 Categories

Let's start by clicking on Categories which will bring us to this screen:

This screen allows us to either create a new category or edit an existing one.

At the top right is our buddy, Screen Options. Let's click it and see what it shows us.

Categories does not have much in the way of screen options by default however be sure to check back here whenever you install a plugin that has anything to do with categories as it may install some new items for you to choose from.

Now let's talk about creating a new category.

Enter a name for the new category in the Name field. Next you can add a slug which is a version of your name that might work better with a web browser. For example if your category name was Two Line Stunt Kites that would be excellent except the spaces will not work well in a web browser so your slug might be two-line-stunt-kites.

If you choose not to manually create a slug, WordPress will automatically create one by replacing spaces with dashes and removing any punctuation.

Now you can use the dropdown box to select the parent of this category. Categories are designed in such a way that they can use a parent-child relationship. What this means is that in effect one can be a sub category of another. Let's look at this using our kite analogy (yes, I fly kites).

Let's say you have a website about kites so your main category (the parent) would be Kites. But there are lots of types of kites so you might have a child category of Single Line Kites. Inside that you might have Delta Kites and Box Kites which are both children of the Single Line Kites parent. Then you could have the Delta Kites broken down into manufacturers so that the Delta Kites category becomes the parent to HQ and Soar kite brand child categories. See where this is going?

This could give us this: Kites > Single Line Kites > Box Kites > HQ where Kites is the main parent with Single Line Kites as a child, then Box Kites is a child of Single Line Kites and HQ is a child of Box Kites.

This hierarchy allows you to have your posts very focused but also allow people to see things as well defined or as broad as they may want.

Next down is the Description box which can include a more detailed description of the category. This description is really only used with some specific themes but can come in handy if you have a lot of esoteric categories.

Once you have all this filled out you can click on the Add New Category blue button at the bottom and the new category will show up in the list of categories on the right side.

The list on the right should look familiar as it is basically the same type of list as the posts list we already looked at just with different columns. The only column that is unfamiliar at this point is the Count column which is the total number of posts in that category.

Clicking on a category title in the list takes us to a page that allows us to edit the Name, Slug, Parent and Description just like when adding a new category.

3.1.1.1.3 Tags

Back to the Posts sub-menu the last item is the Tags item so click on it to get this screen:

This looks just like the categories screen we saw a minute ago except there is no Parent dropdown box since tags do not work in the same parent-child manner. Also note that by default there are no tags in use so nothing is displayed over on the right hand side.

Since tags can be entered at any time while editing a post, I have never actually used this screen to add one, however it is very useful for seeing what tags are in use.

The Screen Options at the top right are exactly the same as on the Categories screen so we won't discuss them again here.

Tags allow you to specify narrowly focused keywords for a particular post. Following our kite analogy this post could be in the Kites > Single Line Kites > Box Kites > HQ category we already talked about but it may have keywords including Blue, Carbon Fiber, and Nylon so people who were searching for blue kites would find it regardless of the category it was in.

Typically you add keywords after writing a post by picking out some useful terms that someone might be searching for. Remember that you can go back and add or remove keywords any time you think you might be able to improve the visitor's experience.

I would warn you about one thing, do not use the same keyword as a tag and a category as this can get confusing not only to your visitors, but to you!

This completes our tour of the posts part of the interface.

3.1.1.2 Media

Just like with posts when you hover over the word Media you will see a fly-out menu you can select items from or you can click the word Media and have those options appear as a sub-menu.

Clicking on the word Media takes you to this screen which is pretty boring since there is no media to display but at least we can talk about the page uncluttered because it will indeed get full in a hurry on most websites.

To start with you have the Add New button so let's click that and add some media.

As soon as you click that button the top of the screen where media would normally be displayed changes to what you see above. At this point you can just drag a picture, document or PDF right into the box to have it uploaded, or you can click the button in the middle that says Select Files. Let's click on Select Files.

This brings up a standard Windows file dialog box (or a Mac dialog box if you are working on a Mac) so you can select one or more files. Once your selection is complete click the Open button to upload the files.

Note that when dealing with images, WordPress can only deal with jpg, png, ico, and gif images. This really should not be a problem as virtually all images you would want to use on a website should already be in these formats anyway.

Now you will see a thumbnail of the file you uploaded, in my case a picture of my MINI Cooper on The Dragon (if you don't know what that is, do an online search for The Dragon Road).

Let's talk about the items on this screen before we click on the thumbnail. Besides the Add New button which we already used there is a white ribbon with some items on it, these are: list mode, grid mode, media type filter, date filter, Bulk Select button and search text box.

List mode displays all your media much like the posts page we already looked at in a list with a small thumbnail on the far left.

Grid mode is what you are already looking at.

The media type filter is a dropdown box that allows you to select All media items, Images, Audio, Video, and Unattached. Selecting one of these options will restrict the displayed list to only those data types.

The date filter dropdown box displays the month and year for each item. If you have ten items in your media library and five are from October 2016, four from June 2016 and one from July 2016 then there will be three options here: June 2016, July 2016 and October 2016. Selecting a month/year from the list will restrict the display of all media types to just ones uploaded that month/year.

Bulk select is a button that once clicked you can click on several media files which highlights them. You will then be presented with a pair of buttons that allow you to cancel the selection or delete all the selected files at once.

Over on the right is a search text box where you can search for media. This search will look in all the text fields associated with the media file and you will see those fields in just a minute when we discuss editing the media.

Click on a thumbnail and you will be presented with a screen similar to this one:

This screen is called the Attachment Details screen and shows you a larger version of the image and a bunch of details over on the right. We will discuss these before talking about the Edit Image button below the image.

On the very top of the page on the right are two arrows and an X. This allows you to move to the previous file, next file and close the attachment details screen respectively.

Below those we have the basic information on the image including the File name, File type, when it was uploaded, file size and the dimensions.

This is followed by the URL which gives you a way to post a link directly to the media from somewhere else such as an email or a forum on another website. You cannot change this so it is grayed out.

Below that is the Title which will be the name of the file you uploaded. In this case the file I uploaded was called buster-on-the-dragon-1.jpg so it got this title (Buster is my MINI's name, yes, MINI drivers name their car, MINI even sends you a nametag to put inside the door well).

Next up is a caption, something that appears below the image when it is displayed on your website. This is not required but can be useful if the image needs a description.

Alt Text comes next and is useful for when your image cannot be displayed or when a search engine wants to know what the image is or when someone is using a screen reader as they cannot read the text. I typically put something like "Buster on The Dragon" here.

The description is just that, a description for the image that usually will not be seen but is useful for search engines and certain themes.

Below that is the person who uploaded the image. For most people this will just be you but on some sites that have a lot of people all contributing information this can be really helpful so you know what belongs to whom.

Below these are three more options: View attachment page (basically a preview page for the image), Edit more details (which is really a view more details page showing image size etc.) and Delete Permanently which does just that.

Now let's click on that Edit Image button below the picture and see what happens.

The first button on the upper left is the crop button but you may notice it is grayed out so you cannot click on it. In order to crop an image you simply click and drag anywhere on the image. Click the left mouse button and keep holding it down as you move the mouse. You will see an area highlighted like this:

Note that a portion of the image has been selected by a dashed box, the rest of the image has been darkened and the crop button in the upper left of the image is no longer grayed out. Clicking that crop button crops the image as shown.

The next button is the rotate image counterclockwise button followed by the rotate image clockwise button.

The following two buttons are the flip image vertical and flip image horizontally buttons respectively.

Now we come to the undo and redo buttons which will be grayed out until you edit an image so there is something that it can undo or redo.

Below the image there is a Cancel and a Save button. The Cancel button simply closes the editor and returns you to the previous screen while the save button (currently grayed out because no edits have been made) allows you to save any changes you make to the image.

Over on the top left you have a left arrow, right arrow and an X which is for previous image, next image and close the image editor respectively.

Below that is the Scale Image function where you can reduce the size of the image proportionally. This means you keep the same exact shape and ratio of length to width while reducing the overall size.

To use this feature simply put a number into one of the boxes. As you do, you will notice the number in the other box changes as you type. Once you are happy with the values simply click the blue Scale button on the right and then either save the image or continue with other editing functions.

Below the Scale Image section is the Image Crop section:

This box works in conjunction with the crop feature we already discussed. When you select a portion of an image the size of the selected area appears in the Selection: area which is grayed out above. This allows you to manually adjust the size of the selection area in pixels instead of by moving the selection box with the mouse.

You can also adjust the aspect ratio by putting in numbers in the Aspect Ratio boxes. Typical values include: 1:1 (square), 4:3 (non-widescreen monitor/TV) and 16:9 (typical widescreen monitor/TV).

As you enter values in any of the boxes under the Image Crop section you can see the selection box on the image change in real time.

The next section, Thumbnail Settings, allows you to change all versions of the image, just the thumbnail of this image, or all the image sizes/uses except the thumbnail. This is really useful for maintaining a square thumbnail and then a widescreen image for larger views. You could also have different crops for thumbnail and several different display sizes (more on that later).

The sub-menu for Media is pretty simple. It includes Library which is where we already started out so nothing new there, and an Add New option which is the same as the Add New button we clicked on when talking about the main Media Library page.

Now that we are done talking about the media library I have one tidbit of wisdom to impart. Never edit images in WordPress if you have any choice. The editing functions are nice to have but a real image editing program (Paint on Windows, Gimp (a free download for most platforms), etc.) will all do a far superior job.

Now when I say a far superior job I don't mean they have more capabilities (which is also true) or that they can do things faster. I mean the end result will LOOK substantially better to the average visitor to your website.

The other concern is that if you were to upload a full resolution image from a phone with say an 8MP camera and then have WordPress reduce the size when it displays it the web page still has to load the entire 8MP file while shrinking the size on the page. This makes for very slow page loads. Always edit and then add it to your WordPress media library.

If we go back to the main Media Library screen and click on the icon in the upper left to switch our view to listing instead of grid we see the following screen:

What is interesting about this particular view is that it shows us where the image is currently being used in the Uploaded To column. If it is being used in more than one place only the first place it was used is shown but this is still a really nice feature to have. Once you have been running a site for a while you can use this to find out what media is not being used anymore and remove it.

I should also mention that there were no screen options for the media screen in grid mode but there are for list mode. Clicking Screen Options in the upper right gives us these options:

If you hover your mouse over an image in the list view you see the following menu appear below the name of the image:

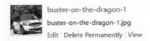

buster-on-the-dragon-1
buster-on-the-dragon-1.jpg
Edit   Delete Permanently   View

Delete Permanently and View are pretty obvious so let's click on Edit and see what happens (hint, NOT what you think).

This edit page is a little different than the other one we have seen as it is missing the tool buttons on the top, the aspect ratio box on the right, and the resize box on the right. What it does have is a box to edit the permalink at the top and more fields if you scroll down:

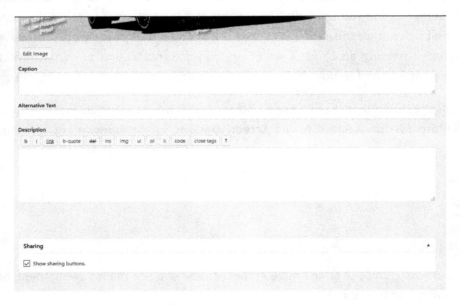

Not only do we have additional details listed (which were also listed in the Attachment Details screen we saw previously, albeit displayed differently) but we have another Edit Image button.

An interesting tidbit is that this is the same page you can get to from the Grid view if you click on an image and on the Attachment Details screen that appears then click on the Edit more details link over on the right hand side.

So let's click on the Edit Image button and see what happens.

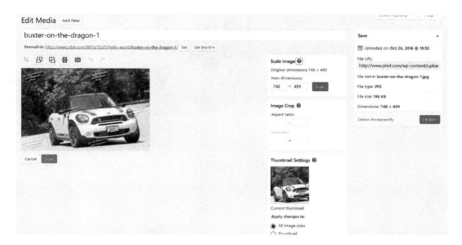

Now there are the options and controls we were missing before! This can be a little confusing to people new to WordPress, especially since so few books and tutorials show you both sets of screens.

Most people pick either Grid or List view for their Media Library and never use the other so they get confused when people who use the other display method talk about their edit screens and they are different.

You can accomplish the same tasks, and edit the same data either way, the information or controls you want may just be on a different screen. I suggest you pick either List or Grid and stick with it to minimize confusion while you are learning.

Later on when you are a WordPress guru you can switch back and forth without missing a beat.

Now there is an easier way to add media to your posts and pages, which is to simply drag and drop it right into the page or post where you want it.

When you do this the screen will change as you drag the image over the post like this:

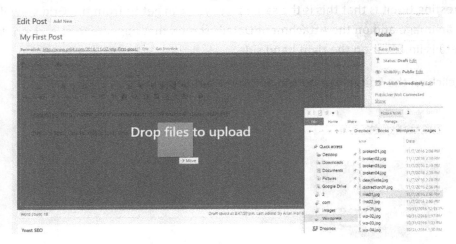

Once you release the mouse and drop the image you will be presented the Insert Media screen:

Here you can select options and click the blue Insert into post button in the lower right corner. The media is now added to your media library and inserted into your post or page.

An important consideration when using media is alignment. This denotes where the text is in relation to an image. For example most of the images in this book have no alignment and are centered meaning that they are in the middle of the page and the text stays on top and on bottom of the images but does not wrap around.

It you look in magazines you will often see images with text wrapped around the side with the image all the way on the left or right hand side of the page.

There are two places to change the alignment: on the insert media page and after the media is inserted into the post or page.

On the insert media page on the bottom right side right above the Insert into post button you should see the image to the left (which is left aligned by the way). If you click the dropdown box you will have four choices: left, center, right, and none. These are in relation to the text so choosing left would make the image on the left side and the text wrap around the right side of the image just like it did above in this paragraph.

Note also that you can add a link to the image or change the image size right here as well.

The other method of choosing the alignment is to click on an image in the post or page editor and use the little menu that pops up like in the image over on the right (that image is right 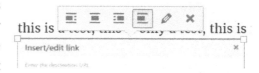 aligned as you might have guessed). The first four little icons are left, center, right, and no alignment.

After the four alignment icons there is a pencil which allows you to edit the image properties and an X which deletes the image from the current post or page but not the media library.

Clicking on the pencil will present the following screen:

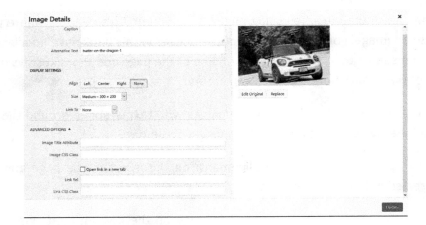

On this screen you can change the caption (text that appears below the image in a post or page like in a newspaper), alternative text (what search engines see and what is read to people with hearing difficulties using screen readers).

Below those are options for changing the alignment, changing the size of the image (including making it a custom size), and linking it to something.

The Link To box provides several options when you click on the dropdown box:

Media File allows you to have a larger version of this image or any other media file (image, audio, video, PDF, etc.) displayed/played/downloaded when the visitor clicks on the image.

Attachment Page takes the visitor to a page containing the full size image of the image on this page when it is clicked.

Custom URL allows you to specify any web address you like. This is useful if you have an item for sale for example on Amazon and when the visitor clicks the image it takes them directly to the sales page on Amazon.com where your item is.

The options under Advanced Options a little further down this page are beyond the scope of this book except for one, Open link in a new tab. While this should be pretty self-explanatory it works in conjunction with the Link To box above and any time a visitor clicks on the image whatever the Link To makes it do, happens in a new tab instead of the current tab.

If you have an image inserted into a post or page and want to move it, you can simply click and hold the left mouse button down on the image and drag it to wherever you want it.

Welcome to WordPress. This is your first post. Edit or delete it, then start writing!

Once it is where you want it, release the mouse button. When you are dragging it around existing text you may notice a vertical line appears in the text where the image will be dropped.

If you want to resize the image manually you can also do that by dragging one of the little squares that appeared on the corners of the image when you clicked on it. While I do not really recommend making a habit of this, and certainly never using it for more than minor adjustments, it is a nice feature to get everything just right.

Audio files (mp3, m4a, ogg, and wav formats) and video files (mp4, m4v, mov, wmv, avi, mpg, and ogv formats) work much the same as the images and have basic players built in.

You may notice that there are files that WordPress will not allow you to upload. These include anything that is not in the specifically allowed list. If you run into this you can simply zip the file and upload it or you can install the WP Extra File Types plugin.

3.1.1.3 Pages

When you click on Pages you may think you accidently clicked on Posts for a second, and indeed they are very similar. In fact, pages and posts differ in so few ways we will only be discussing the differences.

Right off the bat we see that there are fewer columns and filter options. Before we get too far in let's talk about the differences between what a post is and what a page is.

A post is basically a news or blog article. They are generally displayed in date order with the newest at the top and are articles that are usually written on a regular or semi-regular basis.

Pages on the other hand are static and generally have nothing to do with dates.

To get an idea of this you can visit my website at www.allans-stuff.com and look around. The main page and virtually the entire site is made up of pages. The exception to that is if you click on the menu item "ASTRO NEWS/BLOG" at the top right, or look down the right side where it lists "RECENT NEWS".

Clicking on the ASTRO NEWS/BLOG menu shows previews for all the posts in chronological order. As I add a new post it appears at the top. The list of RECENT NEWS on the front page lists the latest five posts in chronological order and as I add a new one it deletes the bottom one and puts the title of the new one on the top.

Other than that Posts and Pages differ because Posts have categories and tags whereas pages do not and pages have an order which can control the order that they appear on menus. Posts do not appear on menus (without a plugin) and so have no order. We will talk a lot more about menus later.

Posts also have excerpts which are by default the first 55 words of the post (this can be changed manually so that you can create your own excerpts for any post you like). These excerpts are used in the feeds along with the title and link to your post which we will cover later.

Pages are great for specific things like a welcome page, contact page, and an about us page. Really any page with content that needs to always be in a specific location on your website would be a good place to use a page instead of a post.

I am kind of an old school guy who likes a website designed primarily through the use of pages however many modern website developers use websites designed primarily using posts. There are pros and cons each way. Find what makes the most sense to you and stick with that until you find a compelling reason not to as just starting out there are no huge benefits either way.

You can also, if you like, create a website that really only contains posts and these are commonly called blogs. We will actually touch on this later.

Lastly, you can specify a particular page as your home page, main page or welcome page. Whatever you call it we are talking about the first page that appears when a visitor goes to your website. We will also discuss that a little later.

We start off talking about the Screen Options on the main pages list view which look like this:

Not a lot here and they are pretty obvious so not much to discuss. Do check back after installing plugins that might interact with pages, especially SEO plugins (more on SEO and plugins later).

That is about all there is to our discussion about pages. If you click on the sample page you will be presented with an editor that looks almost exactly like the posts editor.

Note that the only real differences here are that the category and tag boxes are removed from the right side while the Page Attributes box has been added containing the page order.

This page has no screen options that were not on the post screen options so this will be easy for you. Click Screen Options in the upper right and you should see something like this screen:

Notice that there are a lot that were on the posts that are not here such as Send Trackbacks, Excerpt, and Format. This is due to the different ways that posts and pages are used making some of those items not applicable.

Back at the main page listing page if you hover over the title of a page in the listing it displays a little menu just like in the posts section we already discussed. It contains Edit which is the same as clicking on the title of the page, Quick Edit which we look at in just a second, Trash which deletes the page and View which gives you a preview of the page.

Clicking on Quick Edit shows you the following screen:

Just like on the post's quick edit screen you can turn on and off comments here which I recommend you do for all pages unless you have a specific reason not to.

3.1.1.4 Comments

A comment in WordPress is a reply to a post or page that a visitor writes. You can allow or not allow comments. You can even allow or not allow comments to certain things like yes to comments on posts but no to comments on pages. Restricting where and when we will talk about later but right now let's look at the comments button on our left hand menu.

The first thing you may notice is that there is no fly-out menu when you hover over the Comments option, nor is there a sub-menu when you click on it. This is because comments are a pretty straight forward and simple item.

Our Screen Options at the top right shows us the following options when clicked:

Not much here that isn't pretty obvious but remember that any plugins that have anything to do with comments may put additional options in here so be sure to check after installing related plugins.

Over on the right our list has the same display system as the other portions of WordPress and it all starts out with the Pending (0) | Approved (1) | Spam (0) | Trash (0) display.

Comments work a little differently than posts and pages because they are something that the visitor can do instead of the admin. This is an important distinction because someone could attempt to post something profane, illegal or use your website to advertise their products. Believe me, this is not a matter of it might happen, this is a matter of they absolutely and positively will try this repeatedly.

In fact, here is a comment that was made to my test website (the one we are working with here that has no content except the demo content) that was made while I was working on this book:

This person posted a comment to the Hello World! demo post that was in the default WordPress installation, not one I created. They go on about how great it was, how they will come back to read more, and how great an author I am. They use a Gmail email address, use username of "season 4 of twd" with a YouTube link in their URL.

This is obviously a spam comment on so many different levels that I had to include it to show you what you can expect. Remember, this was on a website with no original content, not yet indexed by a search engine, with no users other than myself. Imagine what happens with more well established and popular websites.

Fortunately there are ways to deal with some of this that we will get into a little bit later.

To help control this, WordPress has a lot of ways built in to stop bad people from misusing the comment feature. The display we just talked about is part of the first line of defense for comments.

When a new comment is made it is Pending. If the administrator likes it they can Approve it, if not they can either Spam it or Trash it. This of course means that the numbers in our display change depending on how many comments we have in each area and that clicking on the name of one of the areas (such as Approved) will limit the list of comments to only those types (such as showing only approved comments).

When a new comment is made on my website I get an email and I can view the comment, approve it or spam it right there. I can also see all the comments that are awaiting approval every time I log into the administration area of the website as they are displayed right on the dashboard.

Below this display is the Bulk Actions dropdown box which allows us to unapproved, approve, mark as spam or move to trash multiple comments. This works by selecting the checkbox next to one or more comments (or all of them by using the checkbox at the very top), using the dropdown box to select the action we want to perform and then clicking the Apply button to the right of the dropdown box.

To the right of that is another dropdown box that allows us to filter the list by either all types, comments or pings.

So what the heck is a ping? Basically an automatic comment that happens when you put a link to another post in your post and that other post has a feature called pingbacks turned on. This is useful when you link to a post on another website as it lets the author of the other article know you linked to them.

Over on the right we have the familiar search box where we can search for a word or phrase in any of our comments.

Now if we look at the list of comments we see there is an author, the comment, in response to, and the date the comment was submitted. The in response to section is just telling you which post or page they wrote the comment in response to.

If you hold the mouse over the comment column you get a little pop-up menu like this:

Comment

Hi, this is a comment.
To get started with moderating, editing, and deleting
dashboard.
Commenter avatars come from Gravatar.

Unapprove | Reply | Quick Edit | Edit | Spam | Trash

Since this comment is already approved you can unapproved it, reply to the author, use either the quick edit or full edit functions, mark it as spam or move it to the trash.

You may have noticed that both the posts and pages sections also did the same thing with popping up a little menu when you hovered over it. On those it was not really that important whereas here it is the only way to really work with comments.

The options to allow you to change the status should be pretty self-explanatory so let's concentrate on the two edit functions. Clicking on Quick Edit gives you this screen:

Note that your screen didn't really change, it just replaced the list portion of the screen with a little mini editor. With this editor you can change anything but the current status which is really not an issue since there are easy ways to do that without being in the edit mode.

Clicking Edit instead of Quick Edit allows you to do the same things, plus change the status as well as give you a lot more room to work.

Note how even though both editors have boxes to edit the same information, these boxes are a lot bigger and give you more room. This comes in handy because the boxes in the quick editor are often too small to display the entire email address or URL which makes it harder to edit.

The quick editor has an Update Comment button over on the right side you need to click once you have completed your editing whereas the full editor has an Update button over on the right without the word "Comment" on it.

Finally if you clicked on Reply on the little pop-up menu you are presented with what looks like a text editor right below the comment you are replying to:

This allows you to directly reply to the comment without having to leave the original comment screen. When done with your comment just click the blue Done button over on the lower right. Your reply will show up as a comment just like any other except in the comment field you will see that it is in reply to an existing comment.

3.1.1.5 Appearance

Let's start the appearance section by discussing what a theme is. A theme is a layout or design to your website. It contains color schemes, font schemes, the general layout and more information that can be applied to the entire website.

By default there are three themes installed in WordPress and these are shown in the screenshot above. Note that each one shows the main welcome page of the website however they are all three laid out differently. You can switch themes and your website will almost instantly be changed to the new theme; every page, every post, every comment, everything.

The really nice thing here is that there are hundreds of themes available, if not more. Many of them are free and there are also some very nice commercial themes. Some themes have free versions and then if you purchase the paid version they enable more features and/or get you support and customization.

Just like several previous areas there is a fly-out menu that converts to a sub-menu when you click on Themes.

Looking at the main Themes screen note that the first theme has a black border around it, says Active before the name at the bottom and has a blue Customize button. Moving the mouse over another theme changes that theme's appearance to look like this:

This action gives you options to see the theme details by clicking the big gray button in the center, activating the theme (applying it to your website) with the white Activate button or looking at a live preview using the blue Live Preview button.

Clicking the Theme Details button presents us with this screen:

This shows us the example screenshot on the left, tells us a little about the theme on the right and then lists a bunch of associated tags on the lower right side. These tags give us an idea of some of the features of the theme such as custom-header and translation-ready in this case.

There are also three buttons on the bottom for Activate, Live Preview and Delete. Live preview is the same as the Customize sub-menu option on the left except it works on this theme instead of the currently active one.

Click the black X in the upper right corner to return to the main themes screen.

Back up at the top of this screen is the number of themes you have installed in the gray circle next to the word Themes, and Add New button we will discuss in just a second and a search installed themes box where you can search through your themes looking for one in particular.

You might be wondering why you need a search feature when there are only three themes and the answer is because a single site might have ten, twenty or more themes as you find ones you like and play with them.

Now let's click on either the Add New button at the top or the Add New Theme dashed box at the bottom and get this screen:

The Add Themes screen starts with an Upload Theme button at the top and clicking that presents you with this:

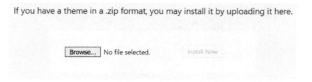

Most people start off by installing themes from the previous screen and we will get there in just a second. This feature allows you to upload a zipped theme from your hard drive. This is important if you want to get a theme from someplace other than WordPress.org, purchase a theme, or if you decide to make your own.

If you have a theme on your computer and want to upload it, click the Browse button here and WordPress will present a standard file dialog box where you can browse and find that theme. Once you select it click Open in the file dialog box and then you should be able to click the Install Now button which is disabled in the previous image. That new theme should now be in the list of available themes for you to choose from.

For now you can click that same Upload Theme button to make the portion of the screen shown in the previous screenshot disappear.

Now we have a stripe across the top which shows the number 15 in a circle which is the number of themes shown on this screen. Note that the word Featured is underlined meaning it is selected, so these 15 themes are the currently featured ones.

Keep in mind that the themes displayed here, as well as the number of themes shown could vary wildly from what I show you to what you see when you look. These can change daily and it can take up to a year or more to publish a book so I would be surprised if they looked very similar.

All of the themes you see here are on WordPress.org. You can be assured that they are safe and completely free. That is not to say that there are not commercial versions of these themes that may have more features, but the ones you can install here do not cost anything.

When you move the mouse over one that is not already installed in your WordPress you will see a screen like the one above showing options for Details & Preview, Install and Preview. The name appears on the bottom left.

You can of course not do the same type of live preview we did previously until you install it but both the Details & Preview and Preview buttons give you a nice big sample screen as well as some information about the theme.

If you like it click the blue Install button and the theme will be installed.

Once installed it will show installed at the top and the buttons change to Activate and Live Preview.

To remove the theme you need to be in the regular themes section. Get there by clicking Appearance over on the far left under Comments and then click on the theme you want to delete (it cannot be the currently active theme), the delete option will be in the bottom right corner.

Let's get back to the Add Themes page. If you are lost, click Appearance over on the far left under Comments and then click the Add New button at the top of the page.

We talked about how the 15 themes here are the ones that are currently featured and we knew that because the word Featured is underlined on the light colored stripe near the top of the page. What do you think happens if we click the next word over, Popular?

Right now when I did it the number 15 in the gray circle turned to 2242 and the underline moved from being under Featured to being under Popular. This is now listing 2242 themes from most popular to least popular. Of course Twenty Sixteen is the most popular as it has been the default for quite some time in WordPress. You will also note Twenty Fifteen and Twenty Twelve right near the top.

Next over on the stripe is Latest which lists the latest themes to be included on WordPress.org. Favorites is an option where if you have an account on WordPress.org you can mark a theme as a favorite and it will show up here. If you don't have an account, or don't want to use this feature that is fine too.

One more to the right is the Feature Filter.

This allows you to filter the list of themes so that the ones listed include the options you want. For example you can select a one, two, three, or four column layout. You could also select one and two column layouts but not three and four. For that matter you can select any combination you want.

When done selecting options click the Apply Filters button at the top left.

Of course there is also the ubiquitous search box at the top right if you want to search the theme names or descriptions for something specific. A good example would be to search for a dark theme or a photography theme.

3.1.1.5.1 Customize

Clicking on the Customize menu option on the far left is the same as we previously talked about, Live Preview. The difference is that Customize works on the currently installed and active theme whereas the Live Preview feature works on whatever theme you click the Live Preview button on. Either way, click on one or the other and you will see a screen similar to the following:

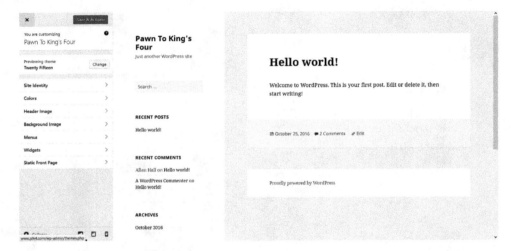

This screen has a menu over on the left for customizing the theme while over on the right is a preview of how that theme will look on your website. Since this is a brand new website and I have done nothing to it the preview is pretty bland and boring.

Let's take a look at the menu on the left. Clicking on Site Identity gives us the following screen:

At the very top is an X to close the preview on the left and a blue button on the right for Save & Activate. Click this button once you are happy with the customization and want to use this theme.

Right below that is an arrow pointing left which allows you to move back to the previous screen. To the right of that is the label for what you are currently working on.

Logo is where you can select an image or graphic to use as a logo for your company or website. Clicking the Select logo button brings up the Add Media box we already talked about in the Media section. Once a logo is loaded it is displayed here and on the preview to the right.

Site Title is where you put in the name of your website while Tagline is a secondary line. A good example would be a site title of "Burger King" and a tagline of "Home Of The Whopper!"

The checkbox for Display Site Title and Tagline is in case you want just the logo image to be displayed without any accompanying text. Your text may already be in the image you want displayed.

The last thing here is the Site Icon which is used as a browser and app icon and must be square and at least 512x512 pixels, but you probably already read that, heh. You can click the Select Image button to bring up the same type of add media box you have used before.

Down at the very bottom of this side you have a triangle pointing left with the word Collapse to the right of it. This is so you can use the entire screen for the preview if you want.

To the right of that are three icons representing a standard computer monitor, a tablet screen and a smartphone respectively. This is so you can see a preview of how the website will look on each of the three platforms.

Click the arrow pointing back and then click on the Colors section to see the screen shown at the right.

The top is the same on all the configuration screens so we will skip all of that and go directly to the Base Color Scheme dropdown box. Dark, yellow, pink, purple and blue are the options presented on this theme and changes not just the single background color but in some cases a contrasting background color for each side of the website. On the left side of this theme is the sidebar while the right side is the general area.

If you want completely custom colors you can start with the Background Color selector which when you click on it opens a color selection box that will allow you to select pretty much any shade of any color you can think of.

The Header and Sidebar Text Color does the same thing as the background color selector and so does the Header and Sidebar Background Color selector.

With these options you can really customize the colors of your website to match anything you can dream up.

The bottom of this section is the same as on the rest of them so we will ignore that. In fact, from here on out we will not show the top and bottom since they are the same on every screen, but instead, just show the center sections which differ on each screen.

Click the back arrow and then the next section which is Header Image.

The header image section is where you can display an image on the header which is basically a banner running across the very top of the page. The recommended size is shown here and I find it is always advisable to resize your image to exactly that size otherwise the image will be distorted. Upload it using the Add new image button here.

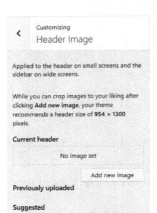

Once uploaded it will show here and of course on the header in the preview pane over on the right.

Click the back arrow and then on the Background Image section.

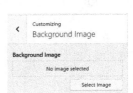

The background image section only has one option, the selection of an image that will appear behind all texts and graphics on the main background. This means only on the right side of this theme.

If the image is too large only a portion will be shown, if it is too small it will be repeated or tiled over and over to fill in the space.

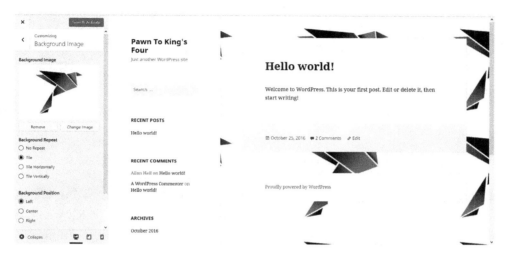

In the screenshot above, the image I uploaded on the left is too small to fill the screen so it is tiled to fill in all available space. Also note that it is only used on the right side.

Note that once I uploaded an image, more options appeared on the panel starting with one which allows us to select how the image repeats if it is not large enough to fill the entire screen. Options here are No Repeat in which case it will only show once, Tile which is what we are seeing here as it is the default, Tile Horizontally meaning it will only tile left to right, and Tile Vertically which means it will only tile from top to bottom.

The next new option is the position of the image which can be Left, Center and Right.

The last new option tells us what will happen when we scroll up and down the page. Scroll means it will scroll up and down with the content on the page while fixed means it will stay in one place as the content moves.

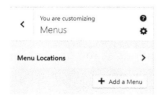

Click the back arrow and then click on Menus to see the next screen.

I never really use the menu options in the theme and in a little while when we discuss the menus in WordPress you will understand why. One part that is useful is on this screen when you click the Menu Locations link and see the screen on the right.

Here you have the option of putting any menu you may have created (and we have not created any yet so there is nothing in the dropdown boxes) in either of two locations. Each theme may have one, two, or even more locations for menus and you do not have to have the same menu in each location.

Click the back arrow twice and then click on Widgets and then Widget Area.

We haven't discussed widgets yet so let's do that before looking at this menu. Widgets are small programs that you can plug in (don't get confused with plugins which we cover in a little while) and then put them in any location that is defined as a widget location.

Widgets can be things that display the latest five posts, list all the categories for posts, display a weather map for your location and much more.

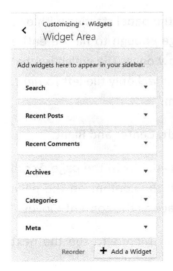

This widget area is populated by several widgets already. Each of the listed widgets can be configured by clicking on the name which opens a menu below that item with options.

For example if you click on Recent Posts a menu opens allowing you to specify a title (Recent Items is the default but you can override that here), the number of recent post titles to display and the option to display the post date.

You also have two buttons at the very bottom to remove the widget completely and close the menu.

On the menu shown above, you have options at the bottom for reordering the widgets or adding a new widget.

All that being said, this is another one of those things I edit in WordPress instead of the theme editor we are in now as it will typically work with any theme.

Hit the back arrow twice and then click on Static Front Page.

By default the top radio button is checked which means the latest post you made is displayed which makes your website look like a blog. If you want to make this more like a typical website you can select the second option of A static page.

Once you have this done there are two dropdown boxes where you need to select things. The first is the Front page box which will be the page, not post, that serves as the first page a visitor sees when they come to your site. Of course right now we don't have a real front page and the only page listed here is Sample Page.

The next dropdown is for the posts page. If your posts don't go on your front page, we need a page for them to go on.

If you look back at my website, www.allans-stuff.com you will see that I have a static front page and my posts page is at www.allans-stuff.com/news/.

3.1.1.5.2 Widgets

Now let's move back over to the sub-menu on the far left. Next on our list to talk about is the Widgets section. Click on the word Widgets and you will see the following screen:

Remember when I said a little while ago that I did not use the widgets section in a theme because there was another place to edit those? This is that place. In fact, at the very top is a button Manage with Live Preview which takes you back to that screen where I said that. Read on to find out why I like it here better.

The left side of this screen shows you your currently available widgets and a little description for each one.

Over on the right side are your widget areas which in this case include a sidebar and two content areas marked Content Bottom 1 and Content Bottom 2. A widget area, or widgetized area, is simply a place in the theme reserved for the placement of widgets. Widgets may only be placed in these specially reserved areas.

There are two ways to move widgets and the easiest is to simply click the left mouse button on one and while holding that mouse button down drag the widget to where you want it. You can drag it from the available widgets area to the sidebar, from the sidebar to the content bottom 2, from the sidebar to the inactive widgets area on the bottom left, or any combination you want.

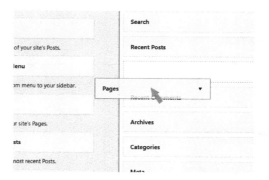

If you want to reorder the widgets on the sidebar you can also drag the top one down two places and then drag the bottom one up to the top. Whatever makes you happy.

The other way to move a widget is to click on the widget and tell it where to go. This works in the available widget area and you can use this to delete widgets from any of the widget areas.

You can also click on a widget in a widget area such as the sidebar to open the configuration page for that widget. When we discussed widgets in the theme customization you could do the exact same thing.

A theme may have multiple locations for widgets and those areas may not be described well such as with our default Twenty Sixteen theme. This theme has three areas: Sidebar, Content Bottom 1 and Content Bottom 2. If you have an issue with where a widget will go simply drag a text widget into the area in question and change that widget's title to the name of the area such as Content Bottom 1.

Now view your website and go to the Hello World! post, then scroll all the way to the bottom where you will see this:

Now you see where the two different widget areas, Content Bottom 1 and Content Bottom 2 are located on your page.

The reason you have to view a post to see these is because they are in "Content" areas, their term for posts which is the primary content of a blog.

This does not mean that there are not widget areas in pages. It is all up to the theme. In Twenty Sixteen the sidebar widget area is available everywhere on the site, not just in posts or pages.

3.1.1.5.3 Menus

Menus are an incredibly important part of your website. If your visitors can not get where they want quickly, they will leave. The average attention span on a website trying to figure out how to do something is just a few seconds. Make those seconds count!

Clicking on our sub-menu item Menus brings up the following screen:

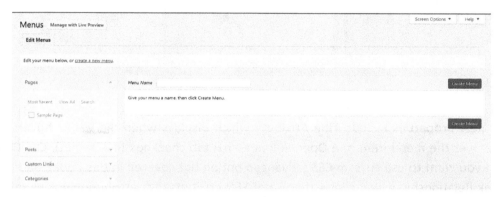

This is another one of those screens that is pretty boring since we do not have anything on here yet but we will change that soon enough.

Our Screen Options in the upper right show us these options when we click on it:

The first four items are already clicked so we will already see those in the items below on the left where we select menu items. Tags and Format add two new items where we can create a menu item that shows all the posts containing a particular tag and in a particular format respectively.

The bottom options labeled Show advanced menu properties show the following items inside the highlighted square on a menu item when enabled:

These new properties include Title Attribute which displays when the visitor hovers their mouse over the menu item, the Open link in a new tab checkbox (link target), CSS Classes should you want to use custom CSS (advanced option not covered in this book), and finally the Link Relationship which allows the use of XFN attributes for attribution linking (also an advanced option not covered in this book).

If you want more information on CSS check out the section Where to go from here near the back of this book. For more information on the XFN linking go to www.WordPress.org and enter XFN in the search box in the upper right corner of the screen.

Closing the Screen Options screen we look at the top of the screen and see the Manage with Live Preview button that takes us to the customization screens. You certainly can manage menus there but I personally find that more confusing.

Since we do not have a menu yet let's enter a name for our menu (I'll use Menu1) in the box roughly in the middle of the page labeled Menu Name and then click the blue button over to the right that says Create Menu.

We now have a screen divided into two sections. The left side has expandable sections for pages, posts, custom links and categories which are the things we can add to our menu.

The right side has a place to display our menu structure and a lower section for menu settings. Let's start by adding a menu item. Click in the checkbox for Sample Page under Pages and then click the Add to Menu button below and to the right of the checkbox.

Now we have a menu item on the right under Menu Structure.

Clicking on the triangle on the right of the Sample Page button drops down a place for us to change the name that will appear on the menu, move the menu item up/down in the menu structure, as well as give us an option to remove this item from the menu. Different menu item types gives us different options such as custom link items having a URL.

You might also note that when clicking on the item you can drag it around. Let's create another menu item and see how this works.

Click on the Posts section over on the left below pages and above custom links. Now put a click to put a checkmark in the box next to "hello world" and then click the Add to Menu button. Over on the right you should see the following:

Now we have two menu items. You can click and drag the bottom one up to the top or click and drag the top one to the bottom. You can also click and drag the bottom one over to the right a little bit to stagger them.

This staggering allows you to make a menu item a sub menu of another item. Let's add one more item and then look at the menu we have created.

Back over on the left click on the Custom Links section right below Posts and above Categories. In the top box named URL it already has "http://" in it, after that type www.yahoo.com and in the Link Text box type "Yahoo!" with the exclamation mark. Now click the Add to Menu button.

Over on the right under Menu Settings click in the box next to Primary Menu and then click the blue Save Menu button over on the right.

If you were to preview the website with this menu, the image above is what you would see. Note that there are two main menu items, Sample Page and Yahoo! while there is a sub-menu item of Hello world! being shown only because I had my mouse hovering over the Sample Page. If I move my mouse the Hello world menu item would disappear.

This is a great way to make nested menus and you can make them several levels deep. Going back to our kite examples I could have a menu for kites and that menu could contain Single Line, Dual Line and Quad Line entries. When you hovered over Single Line it would expand to show Delta, Box, and Diamond entries and then each of those could contain entries for Home Made and Commercial.

Back to our menu settings section we had a couple of other boxes that we did not discuss. The first one is the Automatically add new top-level pages to this menu. I do not use this option because I do not necessarily want a new page to appear on the menu, I may want it somewhere else. Making it automatic makes sense for a very small website but for anything more than a couple pages I leave this turned off.

The bottom option is the Social Links Menu and this is specific to this theme. There are two Theme locations listed here and that can and will change depending on which theme you have. Some themes only have one location and some have two or more. The nice thing is that you can pick and choose where you want the menus and which menu goes where.

Back over on the left we did not look at the section called Categories. This allows you to put a menu option that takes people to all the posts in that category(s).

Back near the top there is a tab called Manage Locations and clicking on it gives you this screen:

Remember that menu locations can change in number, location and name depending on the theme you are using. Some themes have only one menu location while others may have two or more.

With that said, this is where you can assign a specific menu to a specific place, or one menu to multiple places.

Even more interesting than that you can create a menu and put it in a widget.

Go back to the Widget section and notice there is a Custom Menu widget on the left side. Drag that over to the sidebar area on the right and click the downward facing arrow to see these options:

You can give the menu any title you like and then use the dropdown box to select the menu you want to display. Since we only have one menu, Menu1, that is our only option. Once you select the menu and click the Save button the menu should appear on your site.

This becomes useful because you could put a particular custom menu only in this widget. Some uses include all your legal stuff available only from a widget or on the bottom page menu while your top of the page menu has all the navigation selections.

This makes the menu system in WordPress very flexible and powerful by expanding the menu placement options that are included in your theme.

3.1.1.5.4 Header, Background, and Editor

The Header and Background sub-menu options over on the left take you to the header image section and background image section of the customization screen we already discussed.

The Editor section allows you to edit the actual code that makes the theme work.

This section is beyond the scope of this book because it requires you have knowledge of HTML and PHP code. There may however be times when you need to know where this section is so I will spend a couple seconds on it.

The large section on the left is the editor where you can actually edit the code. On the right is the list of files that contain the code you can edit. Scroll down the list on the right until you find the file you need to edit and click on its name, this will open it in the editor.

On most pages when you open a file the bottom will change to add a dropdown box which lists the functions in the code as shown here:

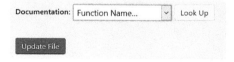

Using the dropdown box to select a function and then clicking the Look Up button launches a web page that tells you about that function. Do not edit the code unless you are sure you know what you are doing. This code is in HTML or PHP and one mistake can stop your website from being accessible or worse, making everything on it appear scrambled.

Later in the book I give you some pointers to where you can learn HTML and PHP and then you *might* think about actually editing the code.

3.1.1.6 Plugins

Plugins are basically little programs or extensions you can get and install in WordPress to provide more functionality or customization. We will be talking a lot about adding plugins later in the book which will cover a lot of specific plugins, but right now let's go over the basics.

Clicking on the Plugins section on the left menu gives us this screen:

This screen should look pretty familiar as it is the same layout we have seen several times before.

Our old friend Screen Options in the upper right shows us these options:

At the top is the Add New button and clicking on it shows you this screen:

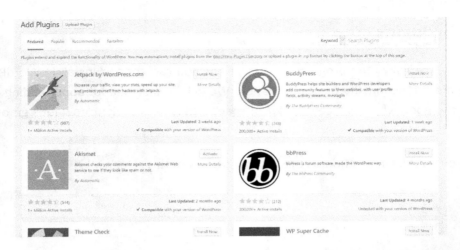

If you are thinking to yourself that this looks just like the themes section you are correct. It works the same too.

At the very top is the Upload Plugin button which presents the following screen:

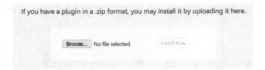

Here you can upload a plugin from your computer. This is really only used if you purchase certain plugins or create your own. When you download free plugins you can do that directly through WordPress.

Back at the Add Plugins screen we have the same type white stripe across the top of the page as we had on the themes page.

The left side contains buttons where we can see the featured, most popular, recommended and our favorites plugins by clicking on that selection. Whichever one has the underline under it is the one we are currently viewing.

Over on the right is the search box we can use to search for a specific plugin by keyword or tag. Keywords can be part of the description or title whereas a tag is something that the author provides in the tag section. For example, you could search for keywords such as backup or speed to find plugins that make backups of your website or increase its speed respectively.

Clicking on one of the displayed plugins pops up a screen with more information such as this:

Here we can see a larger description, when it was last updated, what version of WordPress it is compatible with, how many people have installed it, reviews and ratings and so much more. This is the screen that really helps you figure out if the plugin would help you and your website.

There is an X in the upper right corner you can click to close this window.

Let's actually install a plugin and see how it works. In the search box in the top right type in "Contact Form 7". The list of plugins displayed should change and the one in the upper left should be this:

Click on the Install Now button in the top right corner of the plugin. The button will change to Installing and then finally to Activate. Click the Activate button.

Now we are back at the main Plugins screen with our new plugin highlighted and ready to go. Most plugins (and Contact Form 7 is no exception) require at least some configuration before they really do much and we will cover configuration of this one a little later on in the book.

Looking around at the main Plugins screen (you can get back there by clicking on the word Plugins on the far left if you haven't been following along) we see a lot of familiar items.

Below the Add New button we just explored is the typically styled display All (2) | Inactive (2). This display changes as plugins are added, activated, and deactivated. Clicking on one of the labels in blue restricts the display below to only those types of plugins, such as only ones that are active, only ones deactivated or all of them.

Below that is the Bulk Actions dropdown box allowing you to select one or more plugins by clicking in their checkboxes and then picking an option from the dropdown box (options include Activate, Deactivate, Update and Delete) and finally clicking the Apply button.

You may notice that these same options appear under the name of each plugin although only activate or deactivate exists there depending on the current state of the plugin. Active plugins only have deactivate whereas inactive plugins only have activate.

On the top right is our search box where we can search for a specific plugin which might come in useful as many people tend to install a large number of plugins.

Over on the far left is our sub-menu which contains Installed Plugins (where we are now), Add New (which we already covered) and Editor. The Editor is much like the editor over on the Appearance section where we could edit portions of our theme except of course this allows us to edit our plugins.

Click on the Editor option on the left and you will see a screen like this one:

Over on the top right we can select the plugin we want to work with from a dropdown box by selecting the plugin name and clicking the Select button right next to the box.

Just like themes, plugins typically consist of many files which are listed over on the right side in blue. Clicking on one of these filenames loads that file into the large editor box on the left where you can manually edit the file.

Below this editor window is a Documentation dropdown box where you can select a function used in this file and click the Look Button to be taken to a webpage where it explains that particular function.

Once you are done editing the file you can click the blue Update File button on the lower left of the page to save your changes.

Just like over on the themes section you should not edit these files unless you really know what you are doing as they could not only stop a plugin from working correctly but could potentially prevent your website from working at all or provide a huge security hole that allows you to be infected.

If you want to learn the HTML and PHP code needed to understand and edit these I will put information in the Where To Go From Here section for you.

3.1.1.7 Users

WordPress being as versatile as it is allows us to have more than one person working on a website. You may be the administrator, owner and in charge of everything but you can also delegate things to other people.

The problem here is that you really can't have everyone as equals because people will invariably do things that you didn't want done, or even lock you out of your own website.

To solve this we need to be able to restrict what people can do and this is done with Users.

Clicking on the Users option on the left side menu gives us the following screen:

Let's start by looking in the upper right at our Screen Options by clicking on it which shows us the following screen:

Nothing exciting here however many plugins dealing with users will install new options here for us so we need to make sure we check back after installing user related plugins.

Here we see a familiar screen with the Add New button at the top followed by the All (1) | Administrator (1) display. This display will change as we add more users. Let's do that now, click the Add New button.

The screen that appears allows us to create a new user by entering a Username, Email address, First Name, Last Name, Website, Password and then selecting if you want to send them email about their new account and finally selecting their role on the website.

Only the username, email address and password are required for you to create the user with the default role of Subscriber.

The only real point here to discuss is the role. What is a role and what should you select?

There are five roles: Subscriber, Contributor, Author, Editor and Administrator. Let's talk about each of these.

Subscribers are the lowest form of registered users. This means that the regular visitor who is largely anonymous is the lowest but once that visitor registers with the system they typically start out at a subscriber. Subscribers can read most things, comment on things, receive emails from the system, etc.

Contributors have all the abilities of subscribers but can also create their own posts as well as edit them. They cannot however post them without approval or upload media content.

Authors have all the abilities we already discussed but can also upload media content.

Editors have all the previous abilities and can also publish posts and manage other people's posts.

Administrators are at the top of the food chain and can do anything.

Using this system you can have one or a hundred people working in unison to make your site a success.

Let's start by creating this user with whatever username and password you want and make sure they are set to Subscriber.

Now we see on our main users screen our admin account and the new user we just created. Note that the display below the Add New button has changed to All (2) | Administrator (1) | Subscriber (1) to show that we now have one administrator and one subscriber. Clicking on any of these will filter the list to show only people in those roles.

Below that display we have the Bulk Actions dropdown box and that allows us to select one or more accounts by clicking on the checkbox to the left of their usernames, selecting an action from the Bulk Actions dropdown box (Delete is the only action available on the Users screen) and then clicking the Apply button.

To the right of that is the Change role to dropdown box which allows you to select one or more users, select a role from the Change role to dropdown box and then click the Change button.

Way over on the far right is a search box where we can search for a particular user.

Below this is the list of users showing their username, actual first and last name, email address, role and number of posts they have made. Clicking on a username allows us to edit that user. Click on the new subscriber we created and let's look at the editor screen that follows.

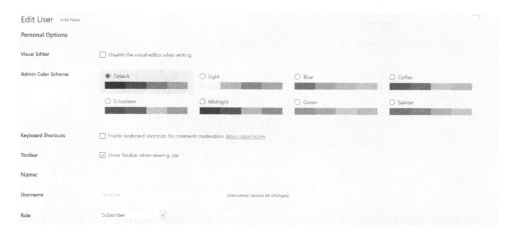

The first portion of the Edit User screen allows us to disable the visual editor with the top checkbox although I have no idea why you would want to do that.

The next section down is the Admin Color Scheme which changes the colors on the admin screens. This really doesn't matter with a user in the Subscriber role as they don't have much access here but for other users it will make more of a difference. The left pair of colors are the backgrounds for the menus while the right pair are the colors for when you move your mouse over an item.

Below that is a checkbox to disable the keyboard shortcuts used in the system. Again, I have no idea why you would want to do this, but here it is.

The next item down is a checkbox to display the toolbar when you are visiting the website and are logged in. That toolbar looks like this:

The toolbar displays at the very top of the website and allows you to access the dashboard and other features directly from this toolbar.

Below that is the username and role dropdown box.

If we scroll down a page we get some new information including the user's first name, last name, nickname, display name, email address, website address and some biographical information about the user.

Moving down the page a little more we have the last few items which includes the profile picture if the user has a gravatar.com account (all avatar pictures in WordPress go through gravatar.com).

Below the avatar is the password change feature where you can either generate a new password or use your own.

Lastly is the Update User button to save the user's information if you changed anything.

There is one difference between other people's accounts and yours, this option at the very bottom right above the Update Profile button:

This option allows you to forcibly log out any machines or devices you may be logged into other than the one you are currently working in. Very useful if you lose your phone, tablet or even laptop.

Looking at the sub-menu over on the far left we see that under Users we have All Users which displays the same screen as if you just clicked on Users above it, Add New which we already discussed in detail and Your Profile which displays the exact same thing as if you had clicked to edit your own profile instead of the new subscriber account we created and edited.

3.1.1.8 Tools

The Tools page is really a legacy option that has not been used since back in WordPress 3 something. It used to work with a technology from Google called Gears however that all stopped back in 2011 when the functionality was pretty much all included in HTML5 eliminating the need for Gears.

What is left in the tools section is Press This which is a way to make it easy to grab text and media from other places on the internet and post it to your site.

The way this works is that you drag the Press This bookmarklet from the tools page to your bookmark bar in your web browser (I know, you probably don't have that turned on but a quick search on the internet will show you how to enable it for your particular browser).

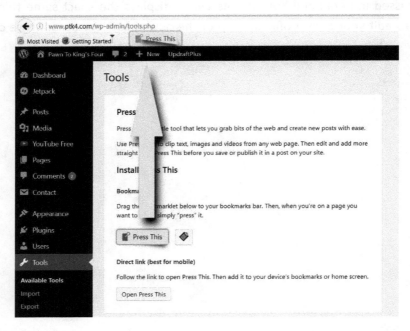

This will install a bookmark on your bookmark bar. Now go visit a blog you like and want to link to your blog. Once you are reading an article you want to quote and link on your blog, click the new Press This bookmark on your bookmark bar and you will see something similar to this:

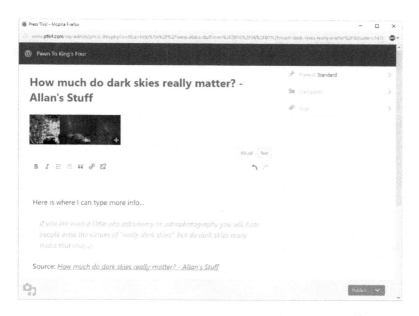

Here is a new post for your WordPress site with the information already in from the post you were just looking at. You are in a little editor where you can make changes, add text, and do other formatting tasks. When you are happy with it you can click the blue Publish button at the bottom right of the screen or click the arrow to the right of that button to get other options such as save draft and go to the full editor.

Additionally the Tools section is where you will find the Import tools which are listed by clicking on the Import sub-menu entry on the far left which displays this screen:

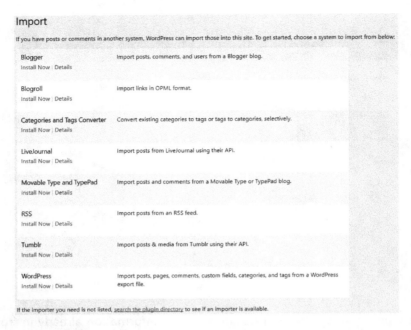

This screen is a list of import plugins which can be installed from right here. In addition, once installed they can be run from right here. Make no mistake however, these are plugins and show up on the plugins screen once installed here. This is just a nice way of listing them for you and allowing you to interact with them from here.

Below the Import selection on the left side sub-menu is the Export selection which displays this screen:

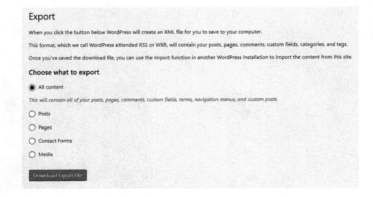

This screen allows you to download in a single file all your site's content, just your posts, just your pages, just your contact forms or just your media.

The first thing you need to know is that this is a single XML file that is downloaded. It contains links to your media files and not the actual media files themselves. For example in this site that we are playing with, the XML file we downloaded includes a link to the picture of Buster on The Dragon but not the actual jpg file we uploaded.

This is normally sufficient if you are planning on using this file to import into another WordPress installation such as moving from one domain to another. It is not however enough if you are thinking of using this as a backup method.

If you click on one of the boxes to select only exporting posts, pages or media you get extra selection boxes such as this example for posts:

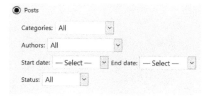

Here you can choose to only export posts for all/specific categories, all/specific authors, all or between specific dates and/or with all/specific statuses.

The selections for pages is similar but of course does not include categories.

Contact Forms has no filters and media only has a date range. Note that contact forms are not included in a default installation of WordPress but we installed the Contact Form 7 plugin which added this to the export tool.

I mentioned briefly about using this to move from one domain to another and you may be asking why. Aside from the obvious reason that someone may want to change their domain name (say they used to be a law firm of Smith, Jones and Doe and then Jones leaves so smithjonesanddoe.com really isn't appropriate any more) it is also common for website developers to set up a website on a temporary site before moving it to a permanent home.

For example I might be working on a website at www.paperbirdtek.com/testweb/ to make sure the customer is happy, or to make sure it is approved by a legal entity (law firms and medical facilities have this problem). Once it is complete and ready for public viewing I can move it over to the customer's domain.

A lot of people might want to just use an "under construction" plugin to keep people from seeing the website and I use those too. The problem with that is that if you have a functional website and want to replace it then the under construction plugin idea doesn't work very well.

3.1.1.9 Settings

The Settings menu option on the left hand menu brings up settings for WordPress and your website that are not handled by themes or plugins. Clicking on the Settings option presents this screen:

Here you can set your site title (the name of your website), a tagline if you want one, the WordPress URL (which can be different than the website URL), the website URL, and the administrator's email address.

Now we see a checkbox for Membership which dictates if anyone can register or not. Unchecked an administrator has to approve a new user's registration but checked they can register themselves. I highly recommend leaving this unchecked.

Remember that visitors do not have to register in most cases (by default) to view any of your published content.

If you elect to allow new users to register themselves the next dropdown box allows you to select the default role for new users.

Below that is the timezone selection for the website and you can either select an absolute time value such as UTC+0 or select a city from a huge dropdown list that is in your timezone. This is used to make sure your posts have the correct time and that you can schedule posts for publication for a later date, and that it actually posts them on time.

Scrolling down further on this same page shows the following information:

Here we can select the date format, time format, the day of the week we want a week to start on and the default language of the site.

Once all your changes have been made you can click the blue Save Changes button at the bottom left.

Over on the left sub-menu you can click on Writing and see the following options:

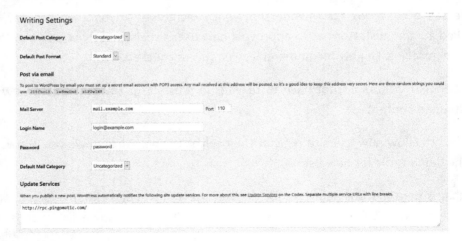

These options have to do with writing, as you would expect. The first option is the category you want posts to be in by default called of course, the default category. If you create multiple categories they will appear in this dropdown box and you can select whichever one you want all posts to be in by default.

This does not mean you cannot change the category of a post when you write it or later, it just changes what happens if you do not opt to choose a category manually.

Way back when we were looking at the post editing screen we talked about formats. This allows you to set a default format. Remember that formats are only used by certain themes.

The next section is for Post via email which allows you to send an email to a special email address you create and that email will automatically be posted to your website.

The first thing you need to do is create an email address. You could do this at gmail.com, yahoo.com, outlook.com or on your own domain if you know how. Once set up you need the information to log in which you will put in the following fields.

Mail Server which could be pop.gmail.com, pop3.yourdomain.com or any number of other options. You need to get this from either the service you set the email up on (gmail, yahoo, outlook) or from whoever hosts your email domain if you use your own domain name.

Login Name is usually your email address but if that does not work contact the service you used to set up your email account.

Password is the password you gave the account when you set it up. All email accounts have passwords, there is no exception to this and never has been.

Default Mail Category allows you to specify a default category for these posts to be in. You might for example have a default category just for everything you send in by email.

Lastly here is a box for Update Services. In website and particularly blogs, people can subscribe to services that aggregates information from several different sites into one readable page or system. This allows a user to look at all the updates to all the websites they like in one place.

These services however do not actually watch your website to see when you make changes, instead they rely on update services to tell them you have updated. These update services in turn rely on you to "ping" them to let them know when something has changed (a new post has been added). This is where you put in the addresses of the services you would like to "ping" when you add a new post.

Below this is a blue button labeled Save Changes.

Now click on the left sub-menu where it says Reading to see this screen of options:

Reading Settings deal with how visitors see your website.

The Front page displays setting we have seen before and dictate if you want your posts to be displayed on the page that first greets visitors like a blog or if you have static pages you want displayed for that like a typical website.

If you select the static page option you then need to use the dropdown boxes to select pages for both the front page (the first page that greets visitors) and posts page (which contains all your posts).

Next you can choose how many posts are displayed per page on your posts page. This means that if you set it to ten and you have between one and ten posts they will all be on one page, if you write an eleventh post it will be moved to a second page with a link at the bottom of the first page to allow users to navigate to the second page. The second page will in turn have a link to return to the first page.

The reason you do not want a high number here is that the more content you cram into one page the slower that page loads. Lower number means more pages but faster page load times. Be sure to balance this with the fact that if your pages are small with little content this will irritate your visitor just as much or more than if your page is slow to load.

Syndication feeds show the most recent is pretty much just like the previous setting of how many articles the blog page shows except this is for your feed.

The feed is a way people can "subscribe" to your news or blog pages. Programs are available to allow people to read all the new content available on multiple websites inside one program instead of having to visit each website individually. This setting controls how many of the latest posts are shown in those readers. I recommend that you leave this at ten.

Every WordPress website has a feed (several in fact, but only one we need to worry about now). That feed is accessible from www.ptk4.com/feed/ on our example website. On yours, simply put /feed/ on the end of the domain name and that is your feed. Go ahead, go check it out, you should see something similar to the following in Internet Explorer, and FireFox while Safari and Edge will ask you what you want to do.

Here you see the only published post on our sample website. If you had more posts it would show up to the number you have defined (default is 10).

Here is one from another of my websites that has more posts:

Note that there are excerpts from each posts and links so that if you are interested, you can click the link to read the entire post.

The next option allows you to display the entire post on your blog page or just a summary. This is a pretty personal decision and may also need to factor in how large your articles are. If your posts are routinely 100-200 words then you might just as well set this to full text. If however your posts normally exceed 1500 words, then you should really consider the summary option as a full text page with ten posts showing all 1500 words each could be a little unwieldy.

The last option is a way for you to stop search engines from indexing your site, assuming they will do what you ask. Most of the major search engines will honor your requests but why would you not want them to index your site? Maybe if it was just a place for friends and family to exchange information and ideas, or a company website for collaboration on products and not intended for the outside world.

Of course after making any changes there is that blue Save Changes button on the bottom left.

Back on the left sub-menu let's click on Discussion.

Discussion Settings

Default article settings	☑ Attempt to notify any blogs linked to from the article
	☑ Allow link notifications from other blogs (pingbacks and trackbacks) on new articles
	☑ Allow people to post comments on new articles
	(These settings may be overridden for individual articles.)
Other comment settings	☑ Comment author must fill out name and email
	☐ Users must be registered and logged in to comment
	☐ Automatically close comments on articles older than 14 days
	☑ Enable threaded (nested) comments 5 levels deep
	☐ Break comments into pages with 50 top level comments per page and the last page displayed by default
	Comments should be displayed with the older comments at the top of each page
Email me whenever	☑ Anyone posts a comment
	☑ A comment is held for moderation
Before a comment appears	☐ Comment must be manually approved
	☑ Comment author must have a previously approved comment

The discussion page has settings related to comments and pingbacks, both of which we covered earlier. Let's take a look and see how we can customize them.

Default article settings has some options that apply every time comments are posted.

Attempt to notify any blogs linked to form the article uses the pingback function we talked about earlier so posts on other websites know when you linked to them.

Allow link notifications from other blogs is part of that same process which allows other websites to notify you when they link to a post on your website.

Allow people to post comments on new articles means that by default when a new post is made, visitors can post comments to it.

Other comment settings include Comment author must fill out name and email which helps cut down on spam and makes sure that people are held accountable for their comments.

Users must be registered and logged in to comment means that there must be a user account active and validated (by whatever means you want) in order for that user to be able to post. Standard unregistered visitors will not be able to comment on posts.

Automatically close comments on articles older than a certain number of days helps prevent people from continuing discussions on old posts. If you have a lot of traffic it can be really frustrating with people looking for answers on posts you made years ago.

Enable threaded (nested) comments means that people can reply to comments and those show up as nested (underneath) the comments. This helps the readers differentiate between a comment on the post and a reply or comment on a comment. In order words, it makes it easier to follow conversations and should be enabled.

Break comments into pages gives you a method to paginate comments if you get a lot of them on a post. If you had a thousand comments and replies it would be unwieldy to have them all in one huge page.

Email me whenever allows the administrator to receive an email whenever someone posts a comment and/or whenever a comment is held for moderation (more on that in just a second).

Before a comment appears allows you to specify that a comment will not appear unless an administrator approves the comment manually or that the comment author must have a previously approved comment. I only check the first box as I want to moderate all comments. Someone could post a very nice comment that really added to the discussion to get approved and then spam your site with horrible comments/advertisements/links with abandon since all their other comments would get automatically approved.

These functions allow you to monitor the comments and only approve real comments while discarding spam comments.

Scrolling down we see more options as shown here:

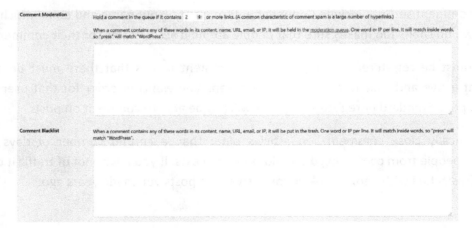

Comment moderation allows you to automatically hold any comment that contains a certain number of links or certain words. This is really helpful at preventing comment spam or comments that contain profanity, etc.

Comment blacklist allows you to automatically trash a comment should it contain any words listed in this box. No moderation, just trashed. You can really make this work well by using a pre-made blacklist here. The one I recommend can be downloaded from https://github.com/splorp/WordPress-comment-blacklist and contains over 23,000 terms current to November 8th 2016 (as I write this on the night of November 11th 2016).

The basic idea is this, go to the link above and read the instructions. In those instructions is a list to the latest blacklist.txt file which you can click on. This loads the text file into your browser. Give it a couple seconds to make sure it is all loaded then press Ctrl+A to select all of the text and then Ctrl+C on your PC or Command+C on your Mac to copy it to the clipboard.

Now open your administration screen and go to the Settings>Discussions>Comment Blacklist and click in the box. Press Ctrl+V on the PC or Command+V on the Mac to paste the text into the box. Wait a few seconds as there are over 23,000 entries and that takes just a little while.

Once the box has filled with the terms scroll all the way to the bottom of the page and click the blue Save Changes button. Done!

Continuing to Scroll down a bit more below the Comment Blacklist section shows these options:

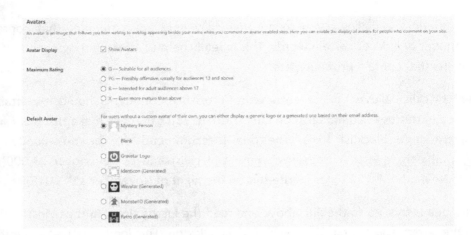

Here you can turn avatars off completely by unchecking the checkbox labeled Show Avatars. This will potentially speed things up if you tend to have a lot of comments.

Next we can change the rating for avatars (this only works with Gravatar) and restricts the avatar the user can use to one that fits in the rating or below.

Default Avatar allows you to set what will be displayed in the avatar place if the user has no avatar with Gravatar.

Below all of this is of course the blue Save Changes button on the lower left.

Back over on the left side sub-menu let's click on Media and get this screen:

These settings allow you to set the defaults for the three sizes that WordPress uses to display images. You can of course set an image to display at any size you want however by default WordPress offers you four sizes: full size, large, medium and small. To make it easier you can adjust those sizes here.

You can also adjust the thumbnail size here which you cannot do anywhere else. You can also uncheck the checkbox under the thumbnail size so that the thumbnail will be exactly the size you specify instead of being reduced proportionally to the approximate size you specify.

Lastly you have a checkbox that allows WordPress to organize your media into month and year based folders for the date you uploaded the media. I highly suggest you leave this checked or you will wind up having a mess should you ever need to find something outside of WordPress (such as with an FTP program).

And of course there is the blue Save Changes button on the bottom left.

Over on the left side sub-menu we can click on Permalinks to see the following:

As we discussed earlier, Permalinks are a way to access content directly using URL friendly links. This means you can grab the URL and paste it into an email program or text message and the person receiving it can click on it and be taken exactly to the post you intended.

These options here dictate how the permalinks are structured and my advice is unless you have a specific reason for changing them, leave the default selection alone as it works quite well.

Scrolling down the page we see some more options:

Optional

If you like, you may enter custom structures for your category and tag URLs here. For example, using `topics` as your category base would make your category links like `http://www.ptk4.com/topics/uncategorized/` . If you leave these blank the defaults will be used.

Category base

Tag base

Save Changes

These options allow you to put prefixes in front of the permalink after the domain portion. There are a lot of options here and you can read the online documentation if you really need custom permalinks.

3.1.1.10 Help system

WordPress includes an excellent help system which is available from the Help tag in the upper right corner and looks like this:

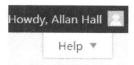

Clicking on it does something similar to this (similar because what is displayed depends on what screen you are on):

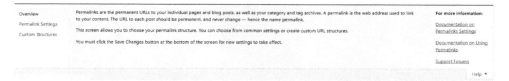

Over on the left we have the overview which is displayed by default and then there is a link for help on each section of the page. Clicking on one of these links changes the information to the right based on the link you click.

This is great for refreshing your memory on what is going on but what if you need a lot more information, not just a summary? See the links on the right side?

Over on the right there is a link for the online documentation (which is excellent) for each section of the page. In addition there is a link below those that takes you to the online discussion forums relating to this topic.

3.1.1.11 WordPress toolbar

When you log into a WordPress site the WordPress toolbar appears at the top of the screen like this:

This toolbar gives us quick access to a lot of things and is particularly useful while viewing the site. Let's take a look at what all we can do starting over on the left side. Move your mouse over the WordPress logo on the far left and this menu will drop down.

Here we can get an About WordPress screen which tells us the current version being used and displays a ton of information about WordPress in general and more specifically this particular version. This can be accessed by clicking "About WordPress" or by just clicking the WordPress logo.

Clicking on WordPress.org takes you to the website for WordPress where you can get a ton of information, participate in forums, download themes and much more.

Clicking on Documentation takes you to WordPress.org as well but more specifically to their codex. The codex is the documentation for all things WordPress and is much more than just a book. Think of it as a book, Wikipedia for WordPress and discussion all rolled into one.

Support Forums again takes you to WordPress.org but directly to the discussion forums where you can get questions answered by other users and programmers as well.

Feedback takes you to the same WordPress forums as Support but drops you off specifically at the Requests and Feedback forum.

Now move your mouse to hover over your website name, in my case that is to the right of the WordPress logo where it has the picture of the house and says Pawn To King's Four.

Clicking either on the top of the menu item or Visit Site that drops down will result in the same thing happening, your website will load just as a visitor would see it except you have the toolbar at the top.

To the right of the website name is a small icon that looks like the boxes you see in comic books that contain the words the characters are speaking. This is appropriate since this represents comments and the number to the right of it shows how many comments are waiting for review. Clicking on the icon or number takes you to the comments administration page.

To the right of the comments is a +New. This displays the following menu when you hover over it:

Clicking the top + New is the same as clicking on Post underneath it and takes you to the new post page.

Similarly clicking on Media, Page or User takes you to the upload media, new page and add user page respectively.

Way over on the far right it will say Howdy, Your Name, hovering over that presents the screen shown on the left.

Here you can click to edit your profile or log out of WordPress.

3.2 WordPress.com

As we already talked about, WordPress.com is a web hosting company that specializes in hosting websites running the free WordPress software. They are especially suited to new users and those with little to no experience in web design or WordPress.

In order to make things even easier for their users they have created a custom interface for WordPress. Many things such as the terms of posts, pages, themes, menus, widgets and plugins are the same; where they are located and what they look like from the administrator's point of view is quite different.

You can get to the full WordPress interface by logging in differently. If you go to www.WordPress.com and click Log In in the upper right corner then you will be given the simplified user interface. If you go to yourdomain.WordPress.com/wp-admin/ (or if you bought a domain name www.yourdomain.com/wp-admin/) and logged in that way then you would get the full interface we have already discussed in the previous section.

In this section I will assume you have read the previous section on using a full WordPress installation as there is no need to cover many of these items twice. I will attempt to touch on differences here and there and cover the basic functionality but will not go in depth as that has already been done.

Let's take a look around the simplified user interface of a WordPress.com website and see what it is like.

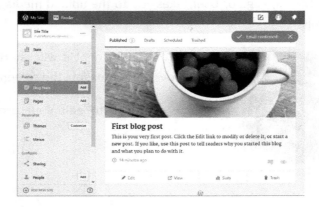

Here is a screen capture from earlier when we set up a new WordPress.com free website. Once the setup was complete we logged in to our control panel which looked like this. If you read through the previous section you may note that the general layout is similar (menu down the left side, toolbar on the top, large display area) but that is about where things stop looking alike.

On the very top left we have a WordPress logo with My Site beside it, clicking on this opens a page in the display area showing how many visitors you have had like this:

Here you can see how active each day a month was, how many views, likes and comments there have been and much more. Scrolling down presents even more information:

Here you see some of information that was displayed on the dashboard of the full installation of WordPress we did earlier such as comments along with more detailed information like followers.

Back over on the left looking at our menus we have the Site Title box with three dots on the far right side of that box. Clicking those three dots changes the box.

Once the box has changed to the one on the right with the gear you can click Edit Icon to change the icon that represents your blog across WordPress.com. Note that this takes you to the full administrator control panel interface for some reason but it does so in a new tab so you can easily close it.

Clicking the gear icon takes you to a page where you can change many of the WordPress settings just like if you were on the full version and clicked on Settings on the menu on the left hand side. There are a few different options and a few options missing but by and large the options remain the same.

Note that the screens are a little different in this layout than they were in the previous sections but mostly the options, labels and boxes remain the same.

Below the Site Title on the far left is Stats which displays the same screen as if we had clicked on the My Site button at the top left as we did earlier.

Below Stats is Plan which in this case shows us Free since I selected the free plan. Clicking on plan shows you the following screen:

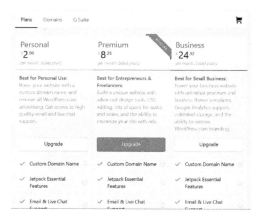

If you think you need more storage space, want to remove the ads, or need other features you can go here to upgrade to a higher plan.

Back over on the left underneath Plan there is a section called Publish that contains Blog Posts (just Posts in the full version) and Pages. Clicking on either one of these presents a list of your current posts or pages.

Down on the bottom of each post you have a little menu that allows you to edit, view, see the stats or delete the post.

Clicking edit of course brings up the editor we already discussed which looks like a streamlined version of the app we already talked about in the full version.

In this editor many of the options we talked about being on the right side of the full version are now on the left, such as categories and tags. There is also a large picture at the top (the featured image) which is different than the full version. Other than those minor changes, everything is very similar in layout and functionality.

Clicking view opens a new tab and gives you a preview of what that post is going to look like.

Stats is very similar to the stats we saw on the main page except it is for just this post.

Trash of course deletes the post.

Pages work very similar except they display in a list as shown here:

This screen lists all the pages you have created. The tabs across the top allow you to filter the list to only show published, drafts, scheduled and trashed pages respectively. You can also use the magnifying glass on the top right to search for specific pages.

Clicking the title of a page opens that page for editing in the editor. There are also three dots over on the right of the title for each page and clicking on these presents a small menu that allows you to view, edit or delete the page.

Over on the left menu you should also see that both Blog Posts and Pages have an Add button on their right hand side. This allows you to easily add a new post or page with one click.

Below the publish section on the left is a Personalize section containing Themes and Menus and both of these sections work very similar to their full version counterparts. I would point out that the themes section here contains quite a lot more themes than the nine that were initially displayed as choices when setting up a new account. It also includes quite a few premium themes which are not free.

Below Personalize is the Configure section which contains several options allowing further customization and configuration of your website. This section includes the following:

Sharing allows you to connect your website with social media sites such as Facebook, Twitter, Google+, and many others. It also allows you to customize the buttons used for linking to those services.

People is where you can add and manage people on your team (people who help you work on your website), and your followers (people who receive email updates when you make a new post).

Plugins is a section much like the plugins area on a full WordPress installation but it is restricted to a handful of included plugins. You can get more plugins by using a paid plan but you are not allowed to upload your own plugins or use any that they do not provide.

The plugin restriction is inconvenient as it imposes some serious limitations, but good from the standpoint of security and stability. Since WordPress.com keeps the list of usable plugins to the ones they provide and verify, you are far less likely to run into problems with plugins not getting along with other plugins or themes. This means less headaches for both the new WordPress user and WordPress.com's technical support department.

Domains allows you to view your domain, add a domain and more. It also has quick access to the plans section since you may need to change plans in order to utilize a new domain name.

Settings we have already discussed as it was the same as clicking on the Site Title dots and then the gear icon. These settings are almost identical to the settings section found in the full WordPress installation.

At the very bottom on the left is a plus sign with Add new site to the side of it. This is the same as if you were on WordPress.com's main website and clicked the blue Create Website button we did in a previous section.

The question mark to the right of add new site brings up the WordPress.com website help.

Over on the top right we have three icons that look like this:

The icons are for creating a new post, accessing settings related to your account and managing your notifications respectively.

Clicking the new post icon simply brings an empty post editor window ready for you to start typing.

Clicking on the middle icon for settings brings up the following screen:

The page you see here allows you to change your name, display name and put in a little bio about yourself. A little further down the page you can also add links such as a link to another WordPress.com page or another website anywhere on the web.

Over on the left there are items you can click on to change the page displayed in the big section on the right. We have been looking at the My Profile section which is what opens by default.

Account Settings allows you to change your username, email address, determine which of your WordPress.com websites is your primary site (yes, you can have more than one), and specify the default language for this interface.

I highly suggest you change your username as right now if you picked a free account your username and website name are the same. In this example my username is mykiteflying and my domain name is mykiteflying.WordPress.com which makes a hacker's job a lot easier as they only need to guess the password.

Manage Purchases is useful if you have a paid account but shows nothing if you are using the free account.

Security allows you to change your password, use two-step authentication, see connected applications and more.

Notifications allows you to specify when WordPress.com sends you a notification. For example when you get a new comment you can have it send you a browser notification and/or an email. You can also manage your reader subscriptions here.

Get Apps provides links to the apps you can download to manage your WordPress and WordPress.com websites. I will cover using the app on a device in the next section.

If you download the desktop app and want to use it for a self-hosted site (one that is not on WordPress.com) you will get this message:

With the app on a device you do not have to install another product such as Jetpack, but if you want to use the desktop app on Windows or Mac then you have to install Jetpack on your website and link it to a WordPress.com account.

Honestly, I see no reason to use the app on a desktop computer as it is just too easy and fast to use a web browser. On a device such as a tablet or phone however the app provides a far superior experience as long as you do not need the ability to work with menus, themes, plugins or configuration settings (this is true for the desktop app too).

Next Steps is like a little to-do list of what you should do after you have your site up and running including Customizing Your Site, Select a Theme, Add a Plan, Start a Post and Create a Page.

Back up at the top right the third and last icon is for notifications and this is where the system will show you notifications, such as new comments, followers, and likes.

This pretty well covers the general layout and functionality of the user interface for WordPress.com. If you need more specific information you can see the previous section on using the full installation of WordPress. In fact, I encourage you to log into your website using the path yourdomain.WordPress.com/wp-admin/ or www.yourdomain.com/wp-admin/ so that you get the full interface.

Not only will the full interface give you more control but since it is consistent with the majority of users out there running WordPress, getting help from anyone who is not on WordPress.com will be much easier.

Of course you do not have to do that right away, go at your own pace. If working with the simplified user interface works for you right now, keep using it until you outgrow it. There is no reason to rush into anything.

3.3 The WordPress device app

Today a large percentage of your visitors will be on mobile, so doesn't it makes sense that you could work on your site using mobile as well? Of course it does!

You certainly can use the web browser on your phone or tablet to log into your WordPress admin panel since WordPress can scale pretty well on devices but there is another option, the app.

This free WordPress app provides a lot of the functionality you need on a daily basis on both iOS and Android platforms. We will be discussing the iOS version installed on an iPad since that is what I normally use. The version for my phone works the same except I find it a little too small to do much work on.

The Android version is very similar and only seems to differ in some of the layout. For example the main icons are on the top of my Android phone whereas they are on the bottom of my iOS phone (yes, I carry both, and I have both types of tablets too, what a geek!).

Start by going to the Apple App Store or Google Play Store on your device and search for WordPress. To make sure you download the right thing, the author should be Automattic. Since it is free you just have to install it and launch it.

The purpose of this app is for you to work with your site's posts, pages and comments. This is a wonderful app for daily use, making posts while on the run, approving comments while waiting in line at the grocery store or fixing a typo on a page while sipping a tall drink on the beach (what am I saying, if you are on a beach sipping a tall drink and even think of working, you need a shrink!). It is not capable of working with themes, menus, widgets, plugins, updates and other core setup functionality.

The first time you launch it, it will ask you to log in with the following screen:

You can create an account for WordPress.com or you can add a self-hosted account (meaning one that is not on WordPress.com). For our example tap the Add self-hosted link near the bottom and the screen will change. (Note that this is the only screenshot in this section from a phone, it is from an Android device I used since I have no accounts set up on it yet.)

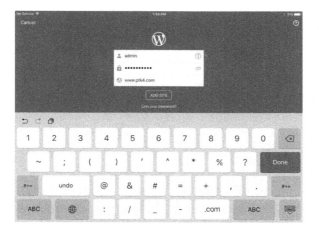

Here I typed in my WordPress admin username, password and the URL to the website. The URL should be the main URL not the direct link to the WordPress administration panel as the app figures that out on its own. In my case I entered www.ptk4.com.

If you entered everything correctly on the previous screen then you should now see the screen above which displays all the WordPress sites you have entered. In my case I have four in the app including the PTK4 one we just added. Note that it pulled the name of the website (Pawn To King's Four) from the site and entered it here.

Tapping on one of the accounts brings up this screen which gives you menu options. I will refer to this screen as the site menu screen. The first of these options is Stats and when you click on it you get the following:

You do not get stats without installing Automattic's Jetpack plugin which we will install in our plugins section. Once the Jetpack installation is complete the stats will display here.

The next option down on the site menu screen is View Site and that simply opens your website in a web browser built into the app.

Below that on the site menu screen is WP Admin which opens your site's WordPress administration page in your default web browser.

Next down is Blog Posts which gives you this screen:

Since we only have one blog post on our example it only shows one, others would be listed below this one in chronological order from newest to oldest.

Below each post are three options: Edit, View, and Trash. These allow you to edit the post, view the post in the built-in web browser and delete the post respectively. Clicking Edit gives you this screen:

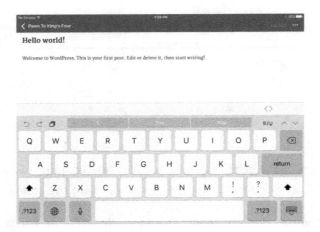

The editor here is not nearly as nice as the editor in WordPress using a web browser but it is more than sufficient for mobile editing and posting. Of course you have your normal keyboard but at the top of that you have a toolbar which allows you to add a picture from your device, bold/italicize/strike text, add a link, add lists, and more.

In addition look at the very top of the screen on the right side and you will see an Update button (grayed out until you make a change) and three dots. Clicking on the dots presents this menu:

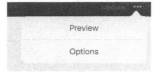

Preview does what you expect, it loads a preview of the post using the built in web browser. The Options button however displays the following screen:

Here you can set the categories, tags, published date, status, visibility, format, set the featured image and set the location. This pretty well covers most of the settings you would normally use in the web version of the post editor. Once done simply click the Back arrow in the upper left corner.

Our next option on the site menu screen is the option for pages. Clicking it shows this screen:

Here you can see all the pages you have created on your site. Clicking on one displays it like this:

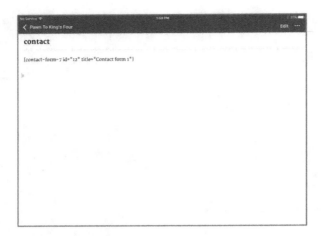

Now you can select Edit from the upper right corner to get the editor screen. The editor for pages is identical to the editor for posts so we won't be discussing it.

The next item down on our site menu screen is comments and clicking on it displays the following screen:

This screen displays all the comments you have which in this case is only two. They are displayed in chronological order with the newest on the top. Clicking on a comment gives you the following screen:

This screen gives you the ability to reply to, approve, trash or mark a comment as spam using the buttons on the bottom of the comment.

The last item on our site menu screen is the Settings option. Clicking on it presents the following screen:

You can change the title of your site, the tagline, the admin password or remove the site from the list of sites in the app from this screen. It also displays the URL and admin username but those cannot be changed here.

Now lets take a look at the buttons on the bottom of the screen as shown in the following image:

The first button, My Sites, takes you back to the first screen you see after login which displays all of the sites you have added into the app.

Next is reader which is basically an RSS feed reader where you can follow blogs and have their new content show up right here. The problem I have with it is that since all my sites are self-hosted that means my WordPress app is not connected to a WordPress.com account, and hence there is no way to manage my feeds. Bummer. Use the Feedly app from the App Store or Google Play store instead.

The next button will create a new post in the last used site. This is a very useful way to add a post quickly.

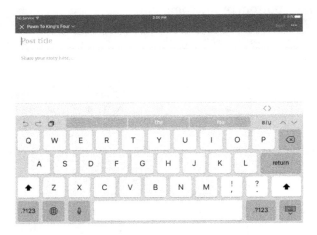

Look in the upper left corner of this editor and you will see a dropdown box that allows you to select the site you want the post to go to, in case you have multiple, and the last one you were in was not the one you wanted to create a post for.

Other than that difference the editor is the same as if you went through a site to create it.

The Me button at the bottom to the right of the new post button brings up the following screen:

Here you have the options of App Settings, Help & Support and Connect to WordPress.com. Clicking App Settings gives you this screen:

This screen allows you to change options about the app itself such as whether to use the visual editor or not.

The Help & Support screen looks like this:

The first option, WordPress Help Center brings this box:

This allows you to search or drill down through topics to find assistance working with the app and your WordPress site. The help in here is surprisingly good for a free app.

The last option you are likely to use on the Me screen is Contact Us which simply brings up a box to send them a message.

Other data on the bottom of the Me screen might be useful in contacting technical support.

The last button on the bottom is Notifications and is another section that only works when you have Jetpack installed.

3.4 The WordPress desktop app

The WordPress desktop app is almost like the device app we just talked about except it runs on desktop operating systems such as Windows and MacOS. The one major difference is that you have to install the Jetpack plugin in order for it to work with self-hosted WordPress sites (anything that isn't on WordPress.com is considered self-hosted by the app).

We will start by opening up the plugins area in your administration area, clicking Add New and then searching for Jetpack.

Once we find the plugin we click to install it and then click to activate it. Once it is running over on the left side menu just under Dashboard will appear a new option, Jetpack. Click on the new option to see the following screen:

If you already have an account simply click the big blue Connect Jetpack box and then type in your username and password to see the following screen:

Now you can click on the blue Approve button and you should be done. What if you don't have an account or don't want to use the same account you use for something else?

On this screen you can click the link at the bottom that says "Sign in as a different user", or on the previous screen you could have clicked on the link "No account? Create one for free…". Either of these two options will take you to a login screen where you can click the Register link below the Log In button.

Here you fill in an email address, username and password for your new WordPress.com account. I will warn you that I have had a problem with some of the "No account? Create one for free…" links in that it would not take me to this page but instead took me to the page where you sign up for a new website instead. Scrolling down and choosing another occurrence of the same link has fixed the issue however. If you get stuck, the direct address to this signup page is https://WordPress.com/start/jetpack/jetpack-user which you can just type into any browser.

Once you fill in the fields and click the button to sign up they will send you a confirmation email with a link in it. Clicking that link will present a login screen where you can enter your newly chosen username and password and log into WordPress.com.

Now you can go back to your administration screen and click on Jetpack on the left side under Dashboard and then click the Connect Jetpack button. This presents the following screen:

Now you can click the Approve button. Once it finishes authorizing the account you will see a plan screen such as this:

Select the free option over on the far left by clicking the Select Free button about half way down the screen. Jetpack is now running and your screen should switch to the Jetpack At a Glance screen inside your WordPress administration screen.

Now we can download and install the WordPress desktop app from https://apps.WordPress.com/desktop/. Once installed, launch the app and enter your username and password we just set up (or your existing one if you want to link to that account instead).

What you see now should look a lot like the redone interface for WordPress.com (not the interface for the full installation of WordPress). You can read more about that in the previous section 3.2 WordPress.com.

If you use WordPress.com as your hosting company (particularly the free hosting) and like the basic interface they offer then this app might be for you. If you are hosting your own WordPress site then this will not offer you all the tools and features you may want.

I tend to use the web interface to all my WordPress websites on a desktop or laptop computer, the app on my devices as we already talked about and on the free WordPress.com installation I use the full administration screen by logging in using the mydomain.WordPress.com/wp-admin/ link.

Your mileage may vary ☺

3.5 The startup sequence, putting all this to use

Now that you have all this information on how things work, how do you put all of that to use with a new WordPress installation? What order do you need to do things in? Does it matter? These are a few questions we will explore in this section.

Starting with the order you need to do things in, there is a general sequence, yes. That should look like this:

1) Decide on what type of hosting you want; managed, unmanaged, full installation, free account, etc.
2) Secure a domain (if you want one) and hosting.
3) Complete the installation of WordPress (either with the host's installer or manually)
4) Configure WordPress for the website (changing names, adding logos, etc.)
5) Start adding content and customizations (plugins, widgets, etc.)

Does this order matter? Yes. If you do not have a hosting service then you cannot possibly install WordPress on your host. Then again, you could in theory reverse steps four and five but that really doesn't make sense as you do not want content in your site if your site doesn't even have a title.

Now we come to a more specific sequence with a lot more steps. This is the sequence I use when setting up a new site and it has served me well for a long time. If something doesn't work well for you, tweak it until it does. After all, it needs to work for you, not me.

1) Decide on what type of hosting you want; managed, unmanaged, full installation, free account, etc.
2) Secure a domain (if you want one) and hosting.
3) Complete the installation of WordPress (either with the host's installer or manually)
4) Log into the new website at www.newdomain.com/wp-admin/ and go to Settings>General. Change the "Site Title" and Tagline. Verify the "WordPress Address", "Site Address", and "Email Address". Set the correct Timezone and click Save Changes at the bottom.

5) Click on Pages>Add New and create a page with the title of "Welcome!". Click the blue Publish button over on the right. Click Pages>Add New again and create a page with a title of News and click the blue Publish button on the right.

6) Click on Pages and delete the sample page (and any pages other than the two we just created).

7) Click on Plugins and delete all default plugins (except Akismet if you intend on using it).

8) Click on Plugins>Add New and add my standard suite of plugins that I always start with (Contact Form 7, Display Widgets, IQ Block Country, TinyMCE Advanced, Updraft Plus, Wordfence Security, and Yoast SEO). Your list will probably be different and will evolve over time.

9) Configure all the plugins I just installed including creating a cloud account such as Dropbox or Google Drive for the backups made by Updraft Plus.

10) Go to Settings>Reading and change the Front page displays setting from Your latest posts to A static page and select Welcome! as the Front page and News as the Posts page. Click Summary under For each article in a feed, show section. Click the blue Save Changes button at the bottom.

11) Click on Settings>Discussion and make sure that "Comment must be manually approved" is checked and that "Comment author must have a previously approved comment" is unchecked. Go to https://github.com/splorp/WordPress-comment-blacklist and open the latest blacklist.txt file, copy and paste that data into the "Comment Blacklist" section of Settings>Discussion. Click the blue Save Changes button at the bottom.

12) Click on Appearance>Themes and delete all but one theme (usually Twenty Sixteen). Install the theme this website will be using and activate it. If the website design I will be using will not work well with Twenty Sixteen then I delete it and find a second theme to use as a backup theme and install it. Configure any options for both the primary and secondary themes so that they can both work with the site correctly.

13) Add content.

14) If this is for a client, contact client and get input on changes/corrections.

This is only a guideline, take it and make it your own.

Section 4: Working with WordPress

Now that we have an understanding of how to install WordPress and how it all works, let's delve into how to make it something usable.

I don't mean to imply anything negative with that statement, it is just that software rarely is what we want it to be right out of the box and needs some customization to do what we want it to do.

The following sections are just that, ways to customize WordPress by adding plugins, using best practices and changing themes. We will use the base install we have already been working with and bring it up to a ready to go website (at least from the back end perspective; images and content are not part of this book, sorry).

What all could there be to customize you might ask? Virtually everything! Not only the way it looks, but the way it behaves as well. In addition we need to make sure it is secure and doesn't fill our inbox with spam on the first day it is online (that, unfortunately, is not a joke).

Keep in mind that if you are using a WordPress.com account or have used the installer on your web host instead of installing from scratch, not all of these may work for you. That's OK, they may have options such as different plugins which do something similar.

Enough, let's get to it!

4.1 Security

Arguably the most important part of a WordPress installation after making it function is securing it. I am not talking about security to keep out the CIA, I am talking about keeping it out of the hands of the thousands of hackers trying to get into websites every day.

That's right, thousands of hackers all over the world are looking for websites they can take control of, alter to advertise their products, infect with viruses and much more. This is a real problem, particularly with installations such as WordPress as they have a standard way of logging in.

Fortunately it is not difficult to provide basic security that will defeat 99.99% of the hackers out there so let's get started!

4.1.1 Best practices

The most important way to secure your website does not require any software, plugins or money, just some guidance and rules. These rules are called best practices.

Let's start when we set up WordPress. If setting up from scratch and you are creating the MySQL databases for your WordPress install make sure that the database name is not something easy to guess. I would recommend you not use WP or DB (or any variation or abbreviation of your website name) as the prefix or beginning of the database name.

A good example is that many hosting providers will tend to use DBxxxxxxxx for the database name for all user created databases and WPxxxxxxxx for the database name when using their built in WordPress installer. Either way this gives the hacker just a little bit of a head start that we don't want to give them. The less they know, the harder their job is.

Next we need to check that your login name is not something easy to guess. We have been working with one of my websites, Pawn To King's Four, www.ptk4.com, so let's continue with that. What would be a good username for me to log in with?

How about we start with what would not be. What would you guess my username is? How about these?

allan
allanhall
allan hall
ah
admin
administrator
ptk4
ptk4.com

All of those are horrible ideas as they are too easy to guess. Trust me, they will try every one of those and even stuff like putting the first name last, etc.

So what can you use? Since the username you log in with does not have to be displayed anywhere you can use anything you want but I highly suggest it be difficult to guess. I might use Jimmy23Beth which might be my next door neighbor's first names separated by a random number. Not likely anyone will guess that.

But what if you already created an account, you can't change the username so now what? Simple enough.

Create a new account with the name you want to use and make sure to set the role to Administrator. Log out as admin (or whatever you used first) and then log in as the new user. Now go into the user editor and change the role on admin to Subscriber. Once you are sure you no longer need the admin account simply delete it.

I would recommend you keep the old admin account around a little while just to make sure the new account does everything you need before you delete the old one.

If you have made posts, pages and comments under the old admin account don't forget to change their author over to the new account.

So now we come to passwords.

The first problem we have is that we should never use the same password at two different places. Sure it makes our lives easier if we only have to remember one password but it also makes the lives of the criminals out to steal our information easier. Since I don't want my information stolen I need different passwords for each use, currently over one hundred fifty of them.

In a perfect world each password would be a randomly generated series of upper and lower case letters, numbers and symbols. Each password would have nothing in common with any other and nothing to do with me. This certainly works well in securing our accounts and is exactly what we should do.

To make this possible one should have a password program that can not only generate these very secure passwords and store them, but also easily copy and paste the passwords into websites as we need them. Since these passwords are random and complex, remembering them and typing them in can be a chore. Fortunately software can make this quite easy.

Another method which is slightly less secure but substantially easier to use is to pick a single complex password and alter it depending on the website you are visiting. For example you could have a password of "u5*wHH!30@?" which is a pretty secure password and then alter it for the website you are visiting. Let's take Amazon.com for example and use the first and last letter of the website and combine this with our complex password to get "ANu5*wHH!30@?". For eBay this would be "EYu5*wHH!30@?" and so on.

This makes it very easy to remember your password for any website and you could even make it more complex by putting something else such as the last two digits of the year on the other end. There are tons of possible variations and this is just a sample of what you could do.

Using this method can be hacked as well because if the hacker gets into one system it is possible that they could catch on to what you are doing. While possible, this is very unlikely as they would have to have access to more than one of your passwords to see the pattern and given that the majority of data breaches tend to result in millions of passwords being revealed it is not likely that anyone will ever go after your password in particular.

If you do decide to use this method do not use the name of the website as that will be a dead giveaway at what you are doing. For example, "amazonu5*wHH!30@?" will be obvious whereas using the first and last letter not so much. You could also use the last two, first two and last one, etc.

So now you have a secure username and secure password, this will eliminate the vast majority of threats you will face because unless someone is looking specifically to hurt you personally, each hacker will only spend a few seconds trying to hack your website and then move on.

Unfortunately there are too many people with easy usernames and passwords for the hacker to spend much time trying to get into any one system unless that system has something really valuable. Let's face it, most of us have nothing that valuable on our websites.

Never write your password down as you might leave it somewhere that someone could gain access to. Your kid, roommate, cleaning lady, the cleaning lady's kid, guy installing your cable TV, how much do you know or trust all of them? What if you put it in your wallet and then lose your wallet? Memorize it or use a password program but do not write it down.

The next items on our best practices list is to remove any themes or plugins that we are not currently using or plan to use. Each one of these items is a potential point that a hacker could use to get into your system and while the odds are pretty low that this will happen, removing things you know you will not be using gives us just that little bit better security making it just a little harder for them to get us.

I do however tend to keep one or two themes around in case things go horribly wrong with my primary theme. If you don't have one installed to fall back on when your primary theme fails (which is very rare unless you are doing a lot of modification or using a very old theme) then it can be substantially more difficult to get things back up and running.

If you have a backup theme then a single click to activate it allows you the time you need to repair your main theme.

Now you might think that you don't need a backup theme because you can just download one really fast, and that is true. The difference is that my backup theme has already been tested with my plugins and although not the exact layout I want, is perfectly acceptable for the website to run for a while.

Speaking of themes, you should always get your themes and plugins from trusted sources. Using the built in functions to WordPress (Appearance>Themes>Add New, and Plugins>Add New) is considered trusted as long as you do not use the upload feature in either place. These themes and plugins come from WordPress.org and are generally well tested and trusted.

There are, of course, other places to get themes and plugins which are very trustworthy, just be sure to do your research before you start downloading and not after you discover a problem. When in doubt you can visit the forums on WordPress.org and ask people where they get their stuff, or ask about a specific places you found interesting items to make sure they are safe.

You should also be wary of where you log into your WordPress website as unsecured networks such as internet cafés and public hotspots could have people watching everything you type though the wireless network. These places are also great places for people to literally watch over your shoulder and see what you are typing.

If you plan on using unsecured or unknown wireless networks and really have no choice, invest in a service that secures everything that is sent/received from your computer. These services as known as Virtual Private Network services (VPNs for short) and are widely available.

Currently my personal choice for a VPN is BlackVPN from www.blackvpn.com. For around $10 per month (or about $100 per year) I get unlimited use on up to three devices including Windows, MacOS, Linux, Android, and iOS devices. I can choose from 18 different servers, all around the world, to make sure I get the fastest and most anonymous connection possible.

This works because when the VPN is active everything I do is encrypted in my computer and then sent through their servers. That data is then decrypted on the other end (let's say I am using their servers in Canada) and sent to where it is going.

This means that websites I visit think I am in Canada and cannot trace my activity back to where I actually am. This prevents anyone who is viewing my network traffic in the internet café from knowing anything except I am talking to some server in Canada. Since everyone on the VPN who is talking through that Canadian server has their data mingled, no one knows whose data is going where, making any data the hacker gets useless.

I should also point out that BlackVPN has multiple ways to connect your machine (Viscosity, OpenVPN, L2TP/IPSec, etc.) and so far has provided excellent support when I needed it.

Many books I have read, and an even larger number of papers online, suggest using the facilities in a security plugin to block or ban IP addresses. This can seem useful because if someone is hammering your login page attempting to enter usernames and passwords in order to get in, banning their IP would stop them permanently, right? The same could work for comment spammers too, right?

Yes, and no. Many of the people attempting these sorts of brute force exploits and spamming attacks are using your typical home internet connection or the connections at their local internet café or school. The problem is that these IP addresses are not static, they change. This means that you may block the IP address and that IP address may be assigned to a completely innocent person tomorrow who legitimately want's to log into your website but is now banned.

Meanwhile the hacker or spammer has a brand new shiny IP address the next day and can continue on until you ban that address as well. This can continue until you have banned hundreds if not thousands of addresses and eventually you start to really make it a problem for real visitors to access your site.

The answer, in my opinion, is somewhere in the middle. Most security software allows for temporary banning of IP address. Generally just a few minutes is all that is really needed but if you want to be sure, go for a day or two. This has the same effect of blocking the spammers and hackers long enough to make them want to move on while making it far less likely that innocent bystanders will get caught in the crossfire.

Lastly, install and use some security plugins and we are going to discuss those next.

4.1.2 Security plugins

While making your username as obscure as possible, and your password as complex as practical is an excellent start to making WordPress secure, there are still a lot of other things to cover.

Plugins are a great way to increase the security of your website since they allow us to add functionality with minimal effort.

What follows are the basic security plugins I use and have found effective over the years. While they are all free, they also offer paid versions. I would recommend you start with the free versions and see if they do what you need. Once everything is working well you can look at the paid versions to see what they offer and decide if you need those features or not.

4.1.2.1 IQ Block Country

My first recommendation does two things: keeps foreign hackers out of your website and prevents a lot of overhead you probably are not aware of. Let's talk a little more about how all this works.

Often hackers will download and use pieces of software that another hacker has written which can automate certain activities. For example there is software that looks at listings of domain names and attempts to log into http://www.yourdomain.com/wp-login which is the default login URL for all new WordPress logins. It then performs attacks using easy username and password combinations, predominately starting with admin and administrator.

This software allows thousands of people to attempt to hack thousands of websites every day. A large percentage of these attacks come from countries such as China, Russia and eastern European countries.

These attacks, even if unsuccessful do cause two problems with your website: slower performance due to constant connections hammering at your login page and excessive logging due to your website constantly writing the information on who is attempting to log in, from where, and using what information into your log files.

Fortunately there is a pretty easy way to stop this assuming you do not need anyone outside your home country from having administrator access. Let me say this again differently to make sure you understand what I mean. This will prevent people from outside your country from logging in to your admin console, not from viewing or interacting with your website.

IQ Block Country is a free plugin which allows you to block people from certain parts of your website. We will be using it to stop people outside our area from being able to attempt logging into our administrator area.

You could restrict people from one specific country, or allow people from one specific country. You could do the same thing for the front end (the part that the typical user interacts with) or the back end (the admin area) or both.

There are a lot of other options here but we will just be using one specific part. Install the plugin and then look under the settings menu on the left side as that is where a lot of plugins put their settings.

When you first get this plugin installed you will receive the following error:

iQ Block Country

The MaxMind GeoIP database does not exist. Please download this file manually or if you wish to use the GeoIP API get an API key from: https://geoip.webence.nl/

Please download the database from: http://geolite.maxmind.com/download/geoip/database/GeoLiteCountry/GeoIP.dat.gz unzip the file and afterwards upload it to the following location: /homepages/38/d161242139/htdocs /ptk4/wp-content/uploads/GeoIP.dat

If you also use IPv6 please also download the database from: http://geolite.maxmind.com/download/geoip/database/GeoIPv6.dat.gz unzip the file and afterwards upload it to the following location: /homepages /38/d161242139/htdocs/ptk4/wp-content/uploads/GeoIPv6.dat

For more detailed instructions take a look at the documentation.

In order for this plugin to work it requires a list of IP addresses and the country they are in. This can change over time so you need to keep this file updated. You have two choices when updating this file: manual or automatic.

Manually updating the file requires you to download the file from the link provided, unzip it and then upload it to the directory specified. I usually do this once every six months or so.

Automatic requires you to purchase a key for 15€ (just over $16) for a year of automatic updates.

The automatic is obviously more secure and easier so if you can afford it, it is a nice option.

If you decide to do it manually just download the file from the provided link, extract the file from the archive (GeoIP.dat) and then upload that file to your wp-content/uploads/ directory.

If you cannot extract the file use a program like 7Zip or WinRAR to extract it. For uploading just use the FileZilla program we used to install WordPress.

Once uploaded click on the settings to see the following screen:

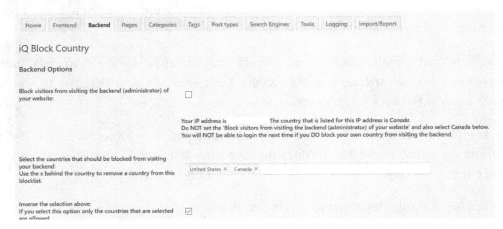

Once you have the settings open, look at the tabs across the top and click on Backend. The options you want to change start with clicking the Block visitors from visiting the backend checkbook and then click in the white textbox next to "Select the countries that should be blocked from..." and scroll down the dropdown list that appears to select the country or countries you want to be able to access the admin portion of your website.

Once you have the countries selected, click the checkbox below this that says "inverse the selection above:" Now click the blue Save Changes button at the bottom of the screen.

That's all there is to making this plugin do what we want.

4.1.2.2 Wordfence

The next plugin I want to recommend is Wordfence Security. This is more of a general purpose security plugin which includes a firewall, malware scan, file checking and much more.

After installation and activation you get this little pop-up over on the left:

Note that unlike many plugins this one puts its own menu item over on the left instead of adding a settings menu to the settings menu (oh that makes a lot of sense, not). Over on the left of the admin screen note there is a menu which we have talked about. In that menu is a section called Settings. Many plugins will add a section under Settings with configuration options for that particular plugin. (Much better!)

You can put in your email address if you like to get information, alerts and general news on Wordfence. You could also start a product tour or just close the window.

Clicking on the Wordfence menu item on the left gives you the basic configuration screen. Across the top will be this banner:

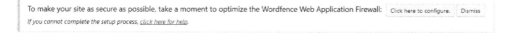

I highly recommend you start with clicking the Click here to configure button over on the right side which brings up this screen:

At the very top is an option to enable an auto-update feature so your security is always up to date.

Next is the server configuration which in my experience is very accurate. If you are comfortable with the selection or just don't know, click the blue Continue button.

At the top of the next screen it complains that I did not enter an email address but it allows me to click the Use My Email Address button to receive email alerts from Wordfence. While I normally am pretty protective of my email address and will even give up discounts instead of giving it out, in this case my website's security is on the line so I click the box.

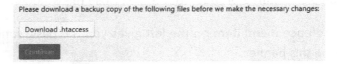

Below that is this portion which wants you to back up a website configuration file. Clicking the Download .htaccess button give you a typical save file dialog box where you can choose where you want to save the file.

Keep in mind that if you have more than one website and they all run Wordfence you will need to save these files under different names or in different places so they do not get confused.

You can now click the blue Continue button.

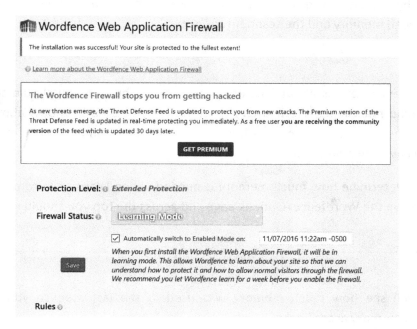

This screen shows you that you are currently in Learning Mode and it will automatically switch to Enabled Mode in a week.

There are a lot more options to Wordfence and even a lot of really cool features with their paid version ($99 per year) if you need some serious security. Rest assured however that installing the free version is a massive step towards protecting your website even if you never opt for the paid version.

There are two notes I should mention with Wordfence: scanning of modified themes causes warnings and larger sites require more memory.

If you use a theme and have modified it (changed the actual code files from what is distributed on WordPress.org) then when Wordfence scans it may report that these files have changed. This is by design. It is trying to let you know of the change so that if you did not make it, and some nefarious person is hacking or hijacking your site, then you need to know about it.

When scanning larger sites I have noticed that Wordfence can use more memory than it is configured by default to use. I have also had cases where your hosting service does not provide enough memory and the scanner runs out.

How much memory should Wordfence request when scanning ⓘ | 256 | Megabytes

In the Wordfence options about 75% of the way to the bottom you should see the line above. I would not change the memory from default (the 256MB shown above was the default on the www.ptk4.com installation I use as an example in this book) unless Wordfence gave you a problem.

To help you determine how much memory is needed, when Wordfence completes a scan you can look on the Wordfence>Options page and across the top you should see something like this:

Wordfence Live Activity: Wordfence used 24.08MB of memory for scan. Server peak memory usage was: 73.97MB

Here you will see how much memory was used in the last scan so you can adjust Wordfence's memory accordingly.

On hosts where Wordfence runs out of memory and they are small websites I have reduced the memory usage to 32MB with good results. On larger websites I have moved it up to 512MB. If you need more memory and your host is not providing enough you can usually call them and ask for an increase. This does sometimes require a higher priced plan however but since it is really only an issue with larger websites that should not be a problem.

Now let's beef up the security of our installation by changing a few options. Click on Wordfence>Options over on you navigation menu and scroll down on the screen that appears until you see the Login Security Options section which looks like this:

What we are trying to do here is to stop, or at the very least heavily discourage, the automated scripts hackers use to attempt to gain access to your site by repeatedly sending username and password combinations.

The first two things to change are the "Lock out after how many login failures" and "Lock out after how many forgot password attempts". Both of these default to 20 which is entirely too many, I prefer 5. This means that after trying to log in five times, and failing all five times in a row, that user's IP address will be locked out and they will no longer be able to attempt login.

The next two options to change are the next two down; "Count failures over what time period" and "Amount of time a user is locked out". Both of these default to 5 minutes and I change the first to 10 minutes and the second to 30. If I am so out of it that I cannot log in after 5 tries in 10 minutes I need to stay away for a half hour before trying again, or go to the doctor's office!

These setting will so dramatically reduce the efficiency of the hackers programs that they generally stop attempts on your site pretty quickly.

Since Wordfence includes protection for the filesystem as well as WordPress itself this can actually cause problems if you tend to install other software alongside WordPress.

A good example is that at www.allans-stuff.com I have a phpBB forum installed for support of my books. The direct URL to the forum is www.allans-stuff.com/forum/. With Wordfence installed with no modifications I can log in and use the forum without issue right up until I attempt to go to the administration control panel where I get a 403 Forbidden error.

The fix for this is to go to your WordPress navigation menu and click on Wordfence>Firewall. Now scroll down to the bottom of the page and look for the whitelist which looks like this:

I manually added the highlighted line at the bottom to fix this problem as Wordfence was blocking access to that file stopping me from logging in. To add a line like this you simply put the relative path from your root directory into the first box marked URL and click the add button over on the far right, no other information is needed.

While you probably will not have a phpBB forum installed on the same server as your WordPress installation, knowing this might help you with a problem with different software.

I found out Wordfence was the issue by simply deactivating plugins until I could log in to my forum's administration control panel. Once Wordfence was deactivated everything worked.

4.1.2.3 Advanced Automatic Updates

Our next plugin solves the problem of updating our software. As you probably know the second most frequent way a hacker gains access to something like a website is through flaws in installed software. Not just WordPress, but your themes, plugins, and anything else.

Just like your operating system (Windows, MacOS, Linux, iOS, Android) and all the software on your computer or device, we need to keep them up to date so when the manufacturer releases patches to fix these flaws, we get them as soon as possible.

The problem is that unless we log in every day and check for updates we could very easily miss important updates. To solve that problem we will use a plugin called Advanced Automatic Updates.

Once you install and activate this plugin look over on the left side under Settings:

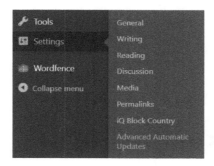

Clicking on the Advanced Automatic Update settings option gives you the following screen:

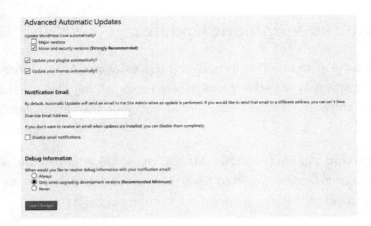

Here you can select options for updating your WordPress installation, your plugins, and your themes automatically. Since major revisions of WordPress can be a pretty big deal I usually recommend you leave that box unchecked and do that manually.

All the rest of the options on this page can be left alone and you can click the blue Save Changes button at the bottom.

Once this plugin is installed and configured we can sit back and relax knowing that all of our software is being kept up to date thwarting the efforts of hackers around the world.

4.1.2.4 Security Ninja

This plugin is a really interesting plugin that checks the security of your WordPress site and tells you what needs to be fixed. I tend to get everything where I want it in regards to security and then install this plugin to see what else I need to do. Once I am done, I deactivate it and delete it.

Go to Plugins>Add New and type Security Ninja in the search box. Look for the following plugin:

Install and activate the plugin. Once activated, it should show you the following popup:

You can click the link in the box to be taken to the Security Ninja page or just navigate to Tools>Security Ninja. You should see something similar to this:

Note the warning about Wordfence being installed. Go to Plugins and deactivate Wordfence and then come back here and click the blue Analyze Site button.

After the scan runs it will show you a screen and tell you what is good, and what is not so good about the security of your website. As you scroll down the page you will see links on the right side of items which you can click on to find out more information on that topic. The information the plugin provides looks similar to this:

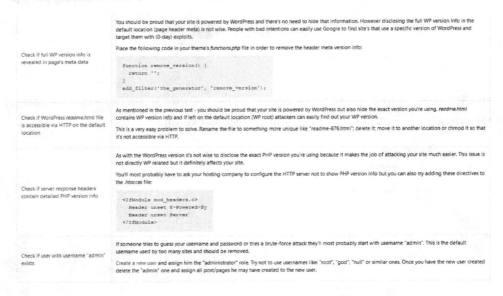

Some of the suggestions could be easy to do, some of them may require editing the actual code base of the WordPress install and therefore may be more than you want to do. You do NOT need to fix everything.

Sure, the more you fix the more secure your website will be, however if you mess something up, that really doesn't help you much does it? Do what you feel comfortable doing and save the rest for a later time when you have more experience and more confidence.

4.2 Extending functionality

One of the greatest features of WordPress is the ability to add functionality through plugins. We have a few plugins thus far but now it is time to ramp things up and teach WordPress how to do some really neat things.

What follows are some of the plugins that I consider mandatory for virtually every website I put together, either for myself or for others. From a single page with a business's contact information on it to a large interactive subscription website, you will find these same ones installed.

I picked these for the book because I always seem to need them and they always just work without causing problems. It doesn't hurt that they are mostly free.

There are hundreds if not thousands of plugins available, most free. While I encourage you to start with the ones in this section I also highly recommend you take some time and search through the available plugins and see which ones work well for you. After all, what works well for me might not be as good for you so explore, play, test and get your feet wet.

4.2.1 Contact Form 7

When we were first talking about plugins and we installed one to see how it worked I had you install Contact Form 7. This was no random pick from the hat, it is one I have running on each and every website I have built.

Just about every website out there presents some way to for you to contact them. Commercial sites want you to purchase something and usually provides product support. Personal sites will often connect you to the owner so you can contribute information or connect with likeminded people. Any way it goes there is usually a way to contact them.

Contact Form 7 makes this really easy. Look over on the far left menu and you will see a Contact section, click on it to see this screen:

Here you see all your contact forms (and the default one the plugin made for you). If you hover your mouse over the name of the form, a little menu will pop up and present you with Edit and Duplicate options. Let's click on Edit.

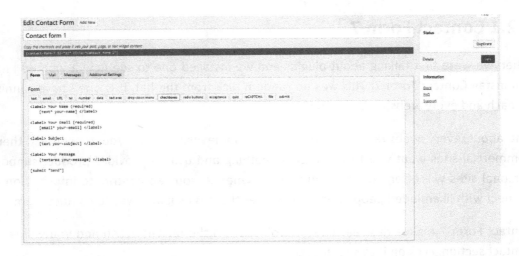

Here is our default form on the Form tab. First up at the top is an Add New button we can use to add another form. This is a nice feature in that you can have a lot of different contact forms. Once we see how we can customize each form you might think of reasons to have several such as one for sales, one for support, etc.

Below the Add New is the form name which you can change, the highlighted shortcode which we will talk about in just a second and several tabs.

The form tab allows you to customize the form that the user sees. Looking at the previous image above you see the code that generates the form the user sees below:

Let's take a closer look at the code and the page.

First up is the shortcode which allows you to copy it and paste that into a page to display the form. That's right, you only have to copy this shortcode into any page, anywhere in that page, to display the form.

Next is the code in the Form tab. Let's look at a line:

```
<p>Your Name (required)<br />
[text* your-name] </p>
```

The <p> portion says this is the beginning of a paragraph and you will note that at the end is a </p> which denotes the end of this paragraph.

The Your Name (required) portion is displayed directly to the visitor.

The <br /> is a line break, telling the form to skip to the next line.

The [text* your-name] part says that what is entered is text and that it is a required field (denoted by the *). This data will be stored in a variable named your-name for later use.

That is the code that is required to create this part of the form:

Your Name (required)

The rest should be pretty obvious now except maybe for the last line:

```
[submit "Send"]
```

This line says that it will create a Submit button and put the word Send on it. The submit button is the button at the bottom of the form your website visitor clicks on in order to send the contact form to your email.

You just learned a little HTML code! Look at you becoming a programmer!

Now let's make sure the form will actually work by clicking on the Mail tab at the top to see this screen:

Most of this is not overly important to start with but you do need to make sure the very top line has your correct email address in it, or at least the correct email address you want the form sent to.

You can also use this page to customize your emails to make them easier for you to read, or easier for you to sort out and put in an automatic filter if you want.

The Messages and Additional Settings tabs are useful for further customization but I won't be covering them because they have nothing to do with getting it to work and so are beyond the scope of this book.

Over on the far left menu below Contact we have Contact Forms which is the listing of our forms we already have, Add New which allows us to create a new form, and Integration.

Integration allows us to add a Captcha into our forms.

The first thing we should discuss is what exactly Captcha is. Captcha is an acronym for Completely Automated Public Turing test, or in layman's terms, a way to tell a human from a computer posting on your contact form.

We need something like this because spammers will use systems that find contact forms and use them to spam you with offers of website promotion, car insurance at great rates and sexual enhancement medications. All of these I already have plenty of so I do not need any more, thank you very much!

Contact Form 7 uses reCAPTCHA from Google and is completely free to use. In order to use it however, you need to get a free key from Google.

To get started with reCAPTCHA go over to www.google.com/recaptcha and click the Get reCAPTCHA button in the upper right corner of the screen.

If you have a Google account sign in here (if you are not already signed in), if not, create a new account or read the section in this book on Analytics for a step by step account setup.

Once you have an account set up and log in Google will tell you that you do not have any sites registered to use reCAPTCHA yet with this screen:

Enter a label in the top box (I just used ptk4.com) and then enter the domain name of your website in the bottom box (again, ptk4.com). Now click the Register button in the bottom right corner.

This screen shows you the two things you need to make reCAPTCHA work: the site key and the secret key.

In your WordPress administration screen go to Contact>Integration and you should see the following screen:

Click the Configure Keys button and the screen should change to this:

Now go to the reCAPTCHA web page and copy each key by selecting it with your mouse and pressing Ctrl+C on your PC or Command+C on your Mac and then pasting that into the boxes for each key here in WordPress by pressing Ctrl+V on the PC or Command+V on the Mac.

Once that is done, click the Save button. You should see a message that says "Settings saved". Now reCAPTCHA is protecting your contact form.

4.2.2 UpdraftPlus

Next up is a very important plugin because it allows us to keep scheduled backups of our website. Can you imagine losing all the time and effort you put into building your website? Are you assuming that your hosting provider keeps backups?

UpdraftPlus is a fantastic plugin that allows you to back up all or part of your WordPress website to a ton of different places including Dropbox, Amazon S3, Microsoft OneDrive, Google Cloud or to an FTP site among other things.

There are a variety of backup options including scheduling in four hour, eight hour, twelve hour, daily, weekly and more.

Now not all of the features are available in the free version, but enough are that you can make real use out of the program. Once you are using it (and completely forget it is even working for you like I often do) then you can decide if you need the premium features from the paid version (starting at $70 for two perpetual site licenses and a year of updates/support).

Start by installing and activating the plugin and then go to the settings page that it puts under the Settings menu item on the far left WordPress menu.

Since this is our first time in UpdraftPlus there is not much to see on the status page. Indeed it tells us that there is nothing scheduled and that no backup has been completed. Let's change that.

Go to the Settings tab which displays this screen:

For the purposes of this installation I will assume you have a Dropbox account and want to back up your website to that. It will work very similar for other solutions.

To start with the main reason I like this program is that I can schedule backups so I don't have to think about them. From the first two dropdown boxes select "Weekly". This should be more than sufficient for most people starting out. As your website grows and gets more popular you may want to increase or decrease the frequency of backups as well as the number of backups being kept.

Next click on the Dropbox logo and name from the list, then scroll down the page.

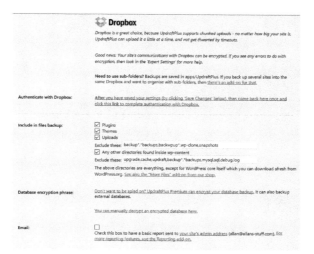

The selections already made are generally fine as they back up pretty much everything. Down near the bottom you see a checkbox where you can have a report sent to your email address showing how the backup went.

Scrolling down a bit further we see:

Here we can show the expert settings which allow us to split the backup archives, delete the local backups, specify the backup directory, and more. I recommend you not alter these settings until you have a firm grasp of how the plugin works and have used it for a while.

Now you can click the blue Save Changes button at the bottom.

After saving a notice should pop up at the top of the screen similar to this:

UpdraftPlus notice: Click here to authenticate your Dropbox account (you will not be able to back up to Dropbox without it).

Clicking on the link provided opens a web page for you to authenticate with Dropbox (or set up a new free account).

Typing in your username and password for Dropbox will cause Dropbox to ask if you want to allow UpdraftPlus to access your Dropbox account:

Now we click the blue Allow button and get this:

And finally we click the Complete setup button at the bottom to be taken back to the UpdraftPlus configuration screen.

Here we can see that the link to our Dropbox account was successful and that scheduled backups are ready to run. We can also click on the Existing Backups (1) tab at the top to see this screen:

This is where we will go to download our backup data if we want a copy on our local computer, restore a backup should something go wrong, delete a backup, or view the backup log to see what was done.

4.2.3 Display Widgets

Display Widgets is one of those things that you just don't understand how that wasn't included in WordPress to start with. I use it all the time.

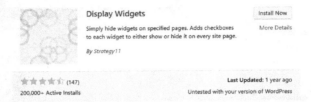

What this simple little plugin does is allow you to display a widget on a page. Wait a second, can't you do that already? Well yes, and no.

You can certainly display a widget on a page. Unfortunately that will display it on every page for every visitor. What if you want different widgets on different pages? Or different widgets for people logged in as opposed to the ones who are not logged in? That's where this plugin comes to the rescue.

A great example might be that you have several subjects on your website and you want different advertisements for different subjects. Or maybe you want no widgets (and therefore no ads) for logged in users. Or maybe one of your widgets is a very useful tool on certain pages (say a weather program for stargazers on your astronomy pages) but having a weather forecast for the middle of the night is not really helpful to people reading your kite pages.

Whatever you decide, this is a really useful plugin. Once you have it installed and activated click on the menu on the left and go to Appearance and then Widgets. Select a widget on the right (I picked Categories) and look at the difference.

On the left is the categories widget before Display Widgets was installed and on the right is after it was installed. See all the extra options?

You can use this to restrict a particular widget to one page, to all pages except one, to posts and not pages, or pages and not posts, and oh so much more. Spend some time looking at the options and I am sure you will agree this is one really flexible tool.

4.2.4 Google Language Translator

Not everyone wants or needs their website translated into tons of different languages. Even if you did have the need, that has got to be expensive and time consuming, don't you think? Well it certainly can be if you need professional level translations but the truth is that most people who need to read the information off most small websites will be perfectly happy with the translations by Google Translate.

But then the user has to go to the Google website and point it back to your page to get it translated, or download a toolbar and use that to get it translated, what a pain! Not anymore.

Download this free plugin and activate it to be able to translate your website into a ton of different languages on the fly for users without the need for them to have a toolbar or visit a third party website.

Once you have it installed there is a configuration page over on the left menu under Settings for Google Language Translator.

Here you see just a portion of all the languages it can translate into. In addition there are a ton of options to customize the look and feel of the way it displays things.

On one of my websites I have it installed as a widget so that I can have that particular widget display at the top right of every single page. I have the plugin restricted to only show six flags which people can click on for an instant translation (the rest are still available from the dropdown box also provided. Here is what that looks like:

Remember that is in the top right corner of every page, small, unobtrusive and very convenient for anyone who needs it.

Scroll down a little on the settings page and we get to see how to make all of this work.

See here the short code (we talked about that earlier) that we can copy and paste in a page or widget. I personally think it works awesome in a widget over on the side of the content but could also see it over the top of a page.

Any way you use it, this is an awesome addition to any website that may have a need for translations.

4.2.5 TinyMCE Advanced

Another plugin that really makes me wonder why it wasn't included by default is the TinyMCE Advanced.

The editor in WordPress is called TinyMCE and this adds a ton of new features to that editor.

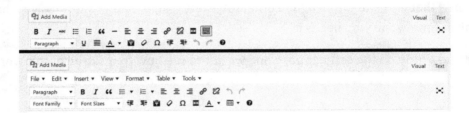

The top is the default menu we have already been working with in the WordPress editor, the bottom is after installing and activating TinyMCE Advanced. Note the menus starting with File, Edit, Insert and so on?

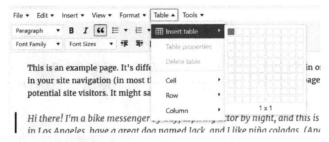

While there are a lot of features here the main one that made me go out looking for something to do this with was tables. Nowhere in the default editor could you work with tables. Sure you could flip over to the text editor and work with them in HTML code but that is a pain in the rear.

Since it is free and does so much, install it and give it a try even if you don't need tables.

4.2.6 YouTube

One thing I was a little disappointed with was the video embedding in WordPress, especially when working with YouTube videos. This sent me looking for something simple and fast.

I wasn't looking for massive control, advertising integration or anything like that. I just wanted something that made adding YouTube videos to my pages and posts easy. This is it.

Installing and activating this little jewel puts a YouTube menu option over on the left menu just under Media (how appropriate!).

It often will pop up this notice when first installed, and later on as updates are released. I am not really fond of this particular update notification feature however it does get your attention.

The one requirement to use this is that we have to have a YouTube account (for you old timers) or a Google account (YouTube and Google are now one, makes life easier). If you do not have one simply go to www.google.com and click on the blue Sign In button at the top right of the screen.

Now click the Create Account link near the bottom and follow the directions.

Once you have an account go to www.youtube.com and log in. On the menu on the top left as seen below click on My Channel.

Then find the video you want to share on your website:

Click on that video which will bring up the video player.

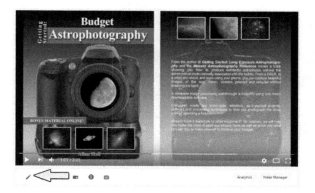

Now click on the Info & Settings icon (the little pencil on the far left side).

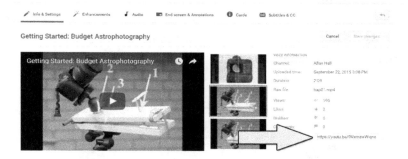

Over on the far right you will see the Video Url which in this example is
https://youtu.be/0VxmzwW-qns and it is this short URL we need to be able to link to. You
can highlight this link and press Ctrl+C on your PC or Command+C on your Mac to copy the
text to your clipboard.

Next open the administration part of your website and open a page or post. In this example
I will be using the "My First Post" post.

At the top of the editor window you should see a new button labeled YouTube, click that.

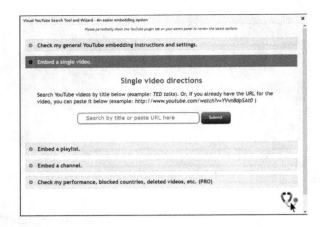

When the screen pops up for the YouTube plugin click the Embed a single video bar to show its dropdown box. Click where it says "Search by title or paste URL here" and then press Ctrl+V on the PC or Command+V on the Mac to paste the URL into the box. Now click the blue button on the right labeled Submit.

Now you should see a screen that shows you a frame from your video. If not, you probably entered the URL incorrectly so go back and copy and paste it again.

Finally you can click on the blue button on the right that says Insert Into Editor. This should return you to your post editor and inserted into the post wherever your cursor was should be a line that looks like this:

[embedyt] http://www.youtube.com/watch?v=0VxmzwW-qns[/embedyt]

You can click Publish or Save Draft depending on what you are working with and then click view the post to see this:

There is my post with my video in a player.

Once you have the plugin activated you can use shortcode to put a link in for a video. Awesome.

For my main website (www.allans-stuff.com) I bought the pro version so I could alter the size and do some other cool things that the pro version has but the free version is still a very capable and easy solution to getting your YouTube videos to appear on your website.

4.2.7 Broken Link Checker

No mystery here, this plugin checks for broken links. That is to say that at some point your posts or pages may have a link to an internal (your own website) or external (someone else's website) that may no longer work. This plugin finds those.

Search for Broken link Checker in the Add New section of Plugins.

Install and activate the plugin. Now you can visit your dashboard and look at or near the very bottom for a box that looks like the following:

Hopefully yours will also show that there are no broken links found but if there are some, you can look at the following screen to see what they are:

Note the new menu item on the left under Tools called Broken Links.

4.2.8 Auto Terms of Service and Privacy Policy

One of the things I hate about websites these days is it seems that unless you are a single page website sharing stuff with only your friends and family you need tons of legal documentation including a privacy policy and a terms of service.

Sure you can just do without it and then worry about whether you should have it or not, or you can just install this little plugin and have your problem solved in minutes.

Go to Add New under Plugins and in the search box type "auto terms". Once you see this plugin:

Install and activate it. You can now click on the Setting link under the name of the Plugin in the listing of installed plugins, or you can look over on your navigation menu under Settings>Auto TOS & PP.

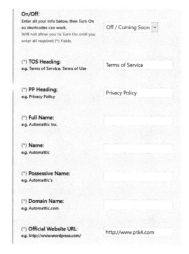

On this screen you need to use the dropdown box at the top and change it to On/Displaying. Now fill in the rest of the form (this image is only part of the form).

Once you have completed the form click the blue Save Changes button at the bottom and then look right above the top of the On/Off button on this page. You should see a listing of available shortcodes like this:

[my_terms_of_service_and_privacy_policy]
[my_terms_of_service]
[my_privacy_policy]

You can highlight one of these and copy it to your clipboard using Ctrl+C on your PC or Command+C on your Mac and then paste it into a page on the website to display one or both the terms of service or privacy policy.

4.3 Working with themes

The theme is the single most important aspect of how your website looks. To make matters worse, there are hundreds if not thousands of choices from which to choose. Then, you can customize the theme using some of its built in controls or even go so far as to make a theme completely from scratch.

A theme is a collection of files that WordPress calls on to tell it how to format text, where to place images, and what color the background should be (among many other things). The Twenty Sixteen theme included with the current WordPress version includes 45 different files.

The basic layout of the website as dictated by the theme which can be illustrated in the following images:

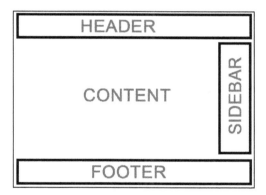

The image above shows the basic layout of a single column theme with the sidebar on the right (that can usually be disabled or moved to the left).

The header is typically where the logo and site name appears and also often contains the menu.

The footer frequently contains widget areas and another menu area.

The sidebars typically contain only widgets.

The content area is normally either a page or posts.

Themes are also classified by columns like so:

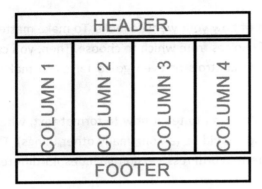 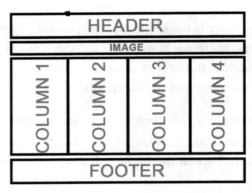

Above are two typical multicolumn scenarios. On the left we have a straight four column layout (themes can have one, two, three or four columns) and on the right is the same basic layout but with an image across the top of all four columns.

These ideas can be combined into all kinds of different layouts. You could for example have a three column design with a right hand sidebar, or a two column design with no sidebar at all.

This needs to be taken into consideration right at the outset so you can pick a theme to fit what you have in mind for your website design, or fit your website to a theme you really like. Either way works just fine.

Once you have an idea what you are looking for you can use the Feature Filter we previously talked about under Appearance to help select a theme that fits your ideas.

Now we come to the other features you can filter by using the Feature Filter and we will go down the Features column and look at a few of them:

Accessibility Ready specifies a theme that is built with an aim towards supporting people with disabilities and their needs.

BuddyPress is a plugin that goes a long way towards converting a WordPress website into a social networking website along the same ideas as Facebook and MySpace. Using this filter will show only themes that would work well with BuddyPress.

Custom Background shows themes where you can have a custom background.

Footer Widgets allows for widgets to be placed in the footer area at the bottom.

Post Formats will display themes that use the Format property in posts.

RTL Language Support provides support for languages that are read right to left.

Threaded Comments shows themes that can provide threaded comments.

As you can see there are quite a few options to choose from so knowing what you are looking for in advance can really help.

The last column in the Feature Filter is the Subject column and shows themes that work well for a particular subject matter. These are completely subjective as what they may classify as a photography theme you might think would be an awesome engineering theme. To each their own.

Themes are stored in the root/wp-content/themes directory and each theme installed has a directory named after the name of the theme. The following image shows the contents of the root/wp-content/themes directory of a default installation of WordPress 4.6.1:

```
   twentyfifteen
   twentyfourteen
   twentysixteen
   index.php
```

Note there are three directories, one for each of the three themes that are included with WordPress. Each directory is named after the theme such as twentyfifteen for the Twenty Fifteen theme.

Each theme has different options and the only way to know if a theme will work for what you want is to try it.

Personally I tend to find themes that give me the general idea I was thinking of and then mold the website to fit the theme. In other words, I have a rough idea of the look I want, choose a theme that looks as close as I can get it, and then blend my mental image of what I wanted with what the theme can do to get a final product.

Section 5: Beyond the basics

So now you have a domain and a web host. You have installed WordPress and learned how to use it. You have even installed some plugins and played with widgets. Now what?

Now we discuss specific topics of things that come up and how to address those issues. The first one is a great example, fighting spam.

While getting the system up and running and learning how to use it is pretty straight forward, some of the issues you run into are not. I should also point out that every issue has a multitude of ways to address it and these are the methods I use. Someone else could use substantially different methods that work as well or better but these should at least get you started on the right path.

5.1 Fighting spam

No matter how obscure you are, someone will find you eventually and spam the heck out of you. It is, unfortunately, unavoidable.

Spam is the unwanted, usually advertising related, posting of comments or of sending you contact form emails. Think of the spam in your email inbox and then apply that to the comments on your board. Yeah, it stinks.

Fortunately there are some things you can do to help mitigate this problem. Note that I did not say eliminate as the only way I know to do that is to turn off comments completely and then remove any way for anyone to contact you through your website, two things we don't want to do.

If however you do want to disable all comments, the best way to do it is to install the free plugin Disable Comments. Go to Plugins>Add New and search for Disable Comments. You should see something like this:

Install and activate the plugin. Go to Settings>Disable Comments and you should see the following screen:

You can either select the top option to disable all comments or you can select the bottom option and select where you do and do not want comments. Click the blue Save Changes button at the bottom and you are done.

Now we can deal with the contact form as that is the easiest. We solved that issue by installing reCAPTCHA which will virtually eliminate robots or scripts from sending us emails (Google is really good at this stuff). Unfortunately it will not stop people from actually filling out the form and going through the CAPTCHA. Believe it or not there are entire companies overseas paying people almost nothing to do this all day, every day, to get past your spam filter.

The next thing we should probably do is install some form of spam fighting plugin such as WP-SpamShield.

Go to your administration screen and then Plugins>Add New. In the search box type WP-SpamShield. You should see the following plugin appear in your search results:

Install and activate the plugin. You're done!

5.2 Analytics

Analytics are a method of measuring and reporting on your website usage. This includes how many visitors you have had in specific amounts of time, what pages they were reading, where they came from, and much more. This information helps us better understand our visitors and aids us in getting more of them.

There are a lot of analytic packages out there but by far the most popular in this department is Google Analytics. Let's set up an account and get it activated on our website so we can start finding out what is going on.

To start off open a browser and head on over to www.google.com/analytics/ and click the Sign In link in the upper right corner. In the menu that appears click on Analytics.

Here you are presented with a screen where you can sign in to your Google account if you have one or click the link below the sign in box that says Create account.

Assuming you are creating a new account you will need to enter your name, email address, password (twice), birthday and mobile phone number.

When you click the blue button labeled Next Step at the bottom you will be presented with their Privacy and Terms policies and you will need to scroll to the bottom before you can click the I AGREE button at the bottom.

Now the service tells you they sent you a verification email which should arrive and look something like this:

Click the link and a page will come up welcoming you to your new account. There is a blue Continue button in the middle of the page, click it.

Now that you have a Google account, or have signed in with your existing one, you are at the analytics signup page so click the big Sign up button over on the right.

The New Account page opens with Website selected at the top. Enter a name for this account under Account Name (I used PTK4 Website). The next box is the Website Name which I entered PTK4. Below that is the Website URL which I entered http://www.ptk4.com. Next I selected Computers and Electronics as my Industry Category and set my Reporting Time Zone to (GTM-06:00 Central Time).

The next section is the Data Sharing Settings which I do not change but those of you who are paranoid about sharing data can uncheck all these boxes and it should not affect your use of Analytics.

Click the blue Get Tracking ID button at the bottom of the page.

Up pops another box with the Google Analytics Terms of Service Agreement which you of course should read and then click I Accept.

Now you are taken to the Admin area of your new Google Analytics account and shown your Tracking ID as in the following image.

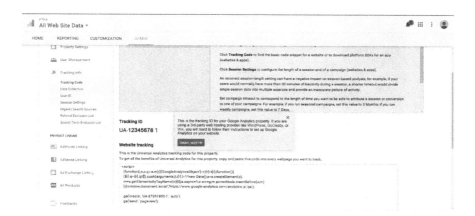

I have of course deleted my tracking ID and put a fake one in there but you get the idea. Notice that there is a box the popped up letting you know you may need to read specific instructions on specific hosting companies to install Google Analytics. We will be using a plugin that should work on any hosting provider assuming you can install and activate the plugin.

Go to your WordPress administration screen and click on Plugins>Ad New. In the search box type "google analytics by monsterinsights" and look for this plugin:

Install and activate the plugin. Over on the left on your navigation menu you should notice a new item below Settings called Insights. If you click Insights you should see a screen similar to the following:

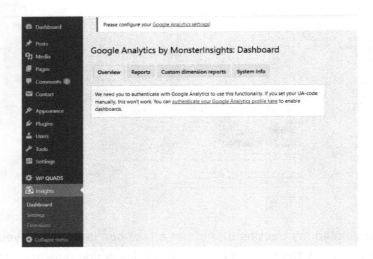

Click the Google Analytics settings link at the very top which will display this screen:

Click the Authenticate with your Google account box which will pop up a pair of boxes. The one on the right lets you sign in to your Google account which you should do.

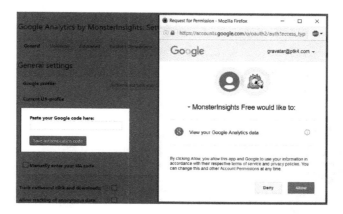

Click the blue button on the lower right that says Allow and the screen on the right will change to something like this:

Click on the line of code and press Ctrl+C on your PC or Command+C on your Mac to copy it to your keyboard and then click in the box in the middle of the screen on the left and press Ctrl+V on the PC or Command+V on the Mac to paste the data in there. Now click the Save Authentication Code button at the bottom of the left hand box and both boxes should disappear and take you back to your administration screen like this:

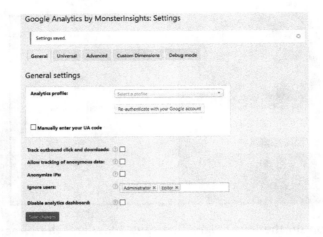

Almost in the middle is a dropdown box next to Analytics profile which says in light gray letters "Select a profile", click that and select the only website you have (mine was PTK4 which is what I named it.

You can of course make changes to the options below but I tend to leave it just the way it is and click Save Changes at the bottom.

You're done! You can click on Insights on the navigation menu to see the dashboard but unfortunately since we just installed the website and just installed analytics, there is no data to see there. The following screen shows what it looks like after it has been running long enough to collect some data:

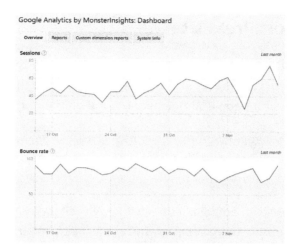

This screen shows traffic and bounce rate by day while clicking on the reports tab at the top presents this screen:

Here you can see how many visitors came from specific places on the internet to get to your website and much more.

While discussing all the ins and outs of Google Analytics is beyond the scope of this book you can find help online at https://support.google.com/analytics/?hl=en#topic=3544906 and for even more in depth information read the excellent *book Google Analytics Demystified* (Third Edition) by Joel J. Davis.

5.3 Moving a WordPress site

We already talked a little about moving a WordPress website in the section on importing and exporting. Now we will cover that a little more in depth. I use this all the time because I tend to develop websites for people somewhere other than their primary domain.

My development usually happens on my www.paperbirdtek.com website with a URL such as www.paperbirdtek.com/clientxyz/. This allows the customer to see and interact with the website as if it was live to tell me what they want added and changed.

The client may have their own domain, let's say it is www.clientdomain.com and very often they already have a website there. That website is usually not a WordPress website so leaving it up with a WordPress site also running on the existing domain is problematic.

Developing on one domain while deploying the finished product on a different domain solves that problem but it creates another problem in that you have to move everything.

We will start at the point at which the new website is complete on the www.paperbirdtek.com/clientxyz/ domain, there is an existing website on www.clientdomain.com which will be replaced and the client has made final approval.

I tend to do this early in the morning on the weekend or late at night on a weeknight so that the downtime of the client's website is not as noticeable.

I will be glossing over specifics on some things but that is because we have already covered much of this in earlier sections. For example I will not tell you exactly what to change in the WordPress config.php file because we have covered that in detail in the section on installing WordPress from scratch.

Start off by logging into ftp.clientdomain.com and download their entire website to a local drive. If their existing website is based on WordPress or another database driven engine such as Drupal or Joomla you need to log into their administration screen and do a backup or export of their database and then download that file as well.

Once you are sure you have a complete backup of their existing website, duplicate it to an external hard drive or USB drive for safe keeping. You cannot have too many backups when you are about to delete everything.

Download and extract the latest WordPress installation files from WordPress.org. Rename the sample_config.php to config.php file.

Set up the new databases for WordPress on the www.clientdomain.com web host and put that information into your config.php file for WordPress.

Connect back to ftp.clientdomain.com and delete all files and folders from the site. Upload the extracted WordPress installation which includes the modified config.php file.

Go to www.clientdomain.com/wp-admin/ and complete the installation and configuration screens. Make sure you use the same administrator username on this install as you did on the demo site as it will make things easier with the import.

Once WordPress is up and running on www.clientdomain.com go back to the administration screen in www.paperbirdtek.com/clientxyz/wp-admin/ and make a list of all the plugins and themes you have installed. Go to Tools>Export and select All content and click on the Download Export File button.

Now go back to www.clientdomain.com/wp-admin/ and install all your plugins and theme, making sure to activate the theme you want. Go to Tools>Import and click on Install Now under WordPress as shown here:

The Install Now link will change to a Run Importer link, click that. On the screen that appears click the Browse button and using the standard file dialog box that appears locate the export file you downloaded in a previous step, select it and then click Open.

On this screen use the dropdown box to select the administrator username which should be the same as the one listed on item 1. Import author. Make sure you click the checkbox next to Download and import file attachments and then click the Submit button at the bottom.

WordPress should now start importing and will notify you when it is done. The last things you need to do are to make any changes to the new installation that you made to the old one. These include any changes to theme options, widget placements, etc.

This method has both good and bad to it so let's take a look at why I do it this way.

The bad is that you have to manually reinstall and configure your themes and plugins as well as make changes to the site title, tagline, etc. You are doing a lot of work over again that could be done automatically with plugins or other utilities to make the move easier.

The good is that invariably when you are working on the demo website you make unintended changes and wind up with more themes, plugins, and media files than you need. This redo of the site allows you to refine what you already did to make the site leaner and cleaner. If you don't need it, don't move it.

I have had a failure of WordPress to import all the media from the old website into the new. For whatever reason it linked the pictures etc. on the new website back to the directories on the old. As soon as I disabled access to the new site, all the pictures disappeared.

To explain this a little better the picture on the old website was http://www.oldsite.com/wp-content/uploads/2016/08/image.jpg. When I did the export and import the address to the image was the same, WordPress did not download it from the old site and upload it to the new site at http://www.newsite.com/wp-content/uploads/2016/09/image.jpg.

In that case I had two choices: I could manually change every link and then manually download and upload all the media files using FTP (not a big deal on most small new sites), or I could wipe out all the posts and pages on the new site and redo the import.

I have only had this happen one time so it has not been a big deal but I did want to make you aware of it. To make sure this does not happen to you, before you completely delete your old website you can simply rename the uploads directory and then check the new website to make sure all the images are still showing up.

Another note of warning is if you do decide to do things this way, make sure any plugins or themes you paid for are registered to the customer's www.clientdomain.com address and not to www.paperbirdtek.com/clientxyz/.

A last parting thought is that I tend to keep the website up (and set to noindex) on my website for a while (like a few months) in case the client comes back with "Why is this like that, I didn't tell you to do that!" you can point them back to the demo website and politely explain that this is what they approved and the new site looks exactly the same. Now if they would like to pay you to make the requested changes, you would be more than happy to help them, meow (Bebay has an attitude, what can I say).

5.4 Search engine optimization

Search engine optimization or SEO as it is usually called is a method or methods to make your website show up higher in search results for a particular search term.

Let's say you were putting together a website on stunt kites and when someone searched for "stunt kites" on a search engine such as Yahoo or MSN you want it to be the first listing they see. Yeah, you and a few million other people, literally.

It is unrealistic to think that you will get to the top listing and unless you have a very unique search term it is unlikely you will even get a first page result.

If I was wanting to score well for stunt kites in Huntsville Texas then I could probably do pretty well as Huntsville is a small town and in my forty years here I have yet to see someone besides myself with a stunt kite.

That doesn't help me if I want to sell kites all over the world however because some guy in Jakarta will not be searching for "stunt kites in Huntsville Texas" so what can I do?

First off if you are reading this book then you have a long way to go before you will be successfully selling a generic product all over the world, but hang in there. If you have a niche product then you might have a reasonable chance (a three line kite or a kite flown by two people at once as these are unique enough that there will not be other sites for them).

So how does a search engine determine rank anyway? That is a moving question because the answer to that constantly changes. As more people "figure out" the system, the search engine operators make changes to break the tricks people employ to get to the top of the list.

One thing does not change however and that is that quality and relevant content rises to the top of the list every time.

What I am trying to say is that there is no long term successful way to game the system or instantly show up in the top links. Anyone who tries to sell you a "secret" or wants you to pay them for a "guaranteed" spot in the top ten or whatever is a snake oil salesman.

If however you put in quality content that people want to read, and do a little work, then you can have a very successful website, eventually.

Quality content means you need to write posts and pages that get and keep people interested. The articles should be approximately 1,000 words at a minimum (this number varies depending on content type however as a general rule it works) and preferably just under 2,000. Anything over 2,000 tends to tire the users out unless it is particularly useful and anything less than 1,000 is seen as non-authoritative.

I also always recommend that you have a relevant picture or two in every article. Some articles, particularly how-tos, should have more. Some articles such as installments on fiction stories may not have any at all or only an illustration every few installments. It varies depending on content but people, and search engines, like images.

The best way for a new webmaster with WordPress to start using SEO is with a plugin. My personal favorite for starting out is Yoast SEO.

With over a million active installs, five thousand reviews and a 4.5 out of 5 star rating they obviously are doing something right.

What I like about it, other than it is free, is that it makes getting the very basics of SEO easy and painless. It will not shoot you to the top of the search engine results but it very well can keep you out of the gutter.

Install and activate the plugin and then go look at the page that lists all your posts.

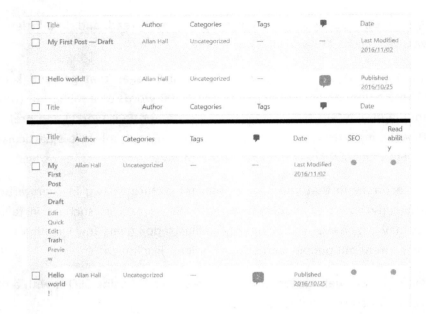

The top part of the image (above the dark black line) is before installing Yoast and the bottom section is after. Note that it now includes SEO and Readability columns.

These columns have little round dots in them which change colors. These colors change depending on how it views your post. Red is bad, yellow needs work and green is good.

The readability column updates whenever you save a new version of a post whereas the SEO requires that you put in a keyword or key phrase for it to measure (more about these in a minute). This gives you a very quick way to make sure that the most basic of SEO has been done and that your pages are readable.

Let's take a look at the post edit screen and see this over on the right side:

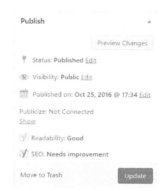

Note near the bottom there are two new lines that start with the Yoast logo: Readability and SEO. They are color coded for easy reading but also tell you what is going on. Looking down below where you normally edit the body of a post shows this screen:

Here you can view and edit your sniplet or excerpt for this post.

Below the sniplet is your focus keyword for this post and it is very important. Choose this keyword with extreme care as it is what all the rest of the settings, suggestions, and indicators will use to tell you how well you are doing with your SEO on this page.

When someone goes on to a search engine and does a search, it should match this keyword. For example if I was writing a post on four line stunt kites I could put that phrase in the focus keyword field and then Yoast will tell me how well the article rates for that particular key phrase.

Below that are some results of an analysis the plugin made with suggestions on how to improve your SEO for this post based on what you put in the focus keyword field above. If you follow as many of the guidelines as you can (without hurting the readability of the piece) then you should substantially increase the quality of your SEO.

Now at the top of this box you will see two tabs with the Keyword WordPress tab as the current one you are on. Click the Readability tab to see something similar to the following:

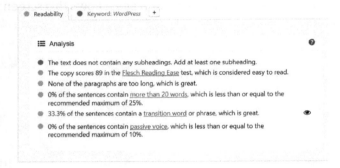

This screen shows you suggestions to improve the readability of the text. Even if search engines did not take this into account at all (which they do) this would be very helpful as it tells you how easy it is for your visitors to read your post, and that is extremely important. Regardless of how good your post is, if your visitors have a hard time reading it, they will move on.

Over on the left side of this area you should see three icons like the ones to the left here. The top icon is where you currently are and is the content optimization portion. The next icon down is the social portion followed by the advanced.

Let's click the social icon to see the following screen:

Here you see where you can put information about your post for sharing on Facebook and Twitter. The information here overrides the title, description, and image that would normally be used to give you a little more control.

Clicking on the advanced icon on the left gives us the following screen:

Here is where you can set whether a spider will index this particular post, whether it will follow links inside the post, give advanced settings to the spiders (beyond the scope of this book), or provide a canonical URL (beyond the scope of this book).

There may be times where you do not want a particular post to show up on the search engines and this is where you can substantially reduce the likelihood of that happening, simply set the first option Meta robots index to noindex.

5.5 Getting images, logos, and more

Once you have the mechanics of your website running (WordPress) you still need to create the content that goes in it. Making that content often requires that you get images, logos, and other media files to put on your site. Generating all that content yourself can be time consuming for some and impossible for others. Let's see if we can get a small jump start.

There is a lot of stuff out there available for free. One distinction you need to make is that free is not always what you want. The reason for this is that free may have stipulations such as you cannot use it on a commercial website or for commercial promotion, or maybe they require a pretty extensive attribution.

Let me start right here by saying this: I am not a lawyer, I do not play one on TV and I did not stay at a Holiday Inn Express last night so take what I say about legal terms with a huge truckload of salt. When in doubt, contact a real attorney.

An attribution is normally where you put something on the image or just below it saying something like "Image courtesy of: Allan Hall, Paper Bird Images" and maybe link the name to their website.

Some people however want a pretty lengthy attribution such as "Image courtesy of Allan Hall, Paper Bird Images, www.paperbirdimages.com, used with permission, Copyright 2016, All Rights Reserved, No duplication or use without prior written permission." Or even more. Sheesh! I certainly want the creator of the image to get what they want in exchange for the image but maybe there is something as good or better that isn't quite so needy.

Ideally you want images, audio, or video that is in the public domain. What this means basically is that you are free to do anything you want with it, generally with the sole exception of claiming you created it to begin with.

You can use it for commercial use, private use, edit it to change it, add to it, remove things from it, whatever you want, without attribution and without payment.

The only things you have to worry about with public domain images are if they have someone in them that is recognizable (meaning if you saw them in real life you could match the image to the person) or if the image has a trademark or copyrighted work in it (such as taking a picture of an iPhone) there could be issues.

So where can you get things like this? The first thing is to just do a search in your favorite search engine for public domain images. Do be careful however because not all images, or websites full of images that come up will have public domain images in them. Some people have commercial websites and populate it with the public domain keyword so you will find it and just pay for images. Not cool but they do exist.

The next place to look is government archives. Most government agencies as far as I know in the United States release images they take into the public domain. After all, we taxpayers already paid for them once, right?

You can also go to NASA and download a ton of space related images and use them all. Awesome. You would be really surprised to find out what all the US government has pictures of. Need pictures of national parks, no problem, how about Hoover dam, plenty of them.

Another thing to be wary of is places that have public domain images in one resolution but offer the same image as a "premium" image in that it is at a higher resolution when you pay for it. These same sites may offer paid non-public domain images on the same page as the public domain images. Let's take a look at one as an example.

This is an excellent website with some nice public domain images. They are doing absolutely nothing wrong by offering both public domain and non-public domain images on the same page, it is just something you need to be aware of.

In this case the public domain version of the image of the sheet music is 1280 x 960 in resolution. More than enough to put on any website and even to print in a book if you size it at around 4" wide.

The premium version of this image is 4000 x 3000 in resolution and is better suited to a magazine or book cover, billboard, or an image you print out to hang on the wall, all uses you should not have a problem paying a small fee for.

If you want a place to start looking at images, try www.pixnio.com, www.publicdomainpictures.net, and commons.wikimedia.org.

Now let's say you had a website that needed really nice images. Sure there are some really nice public domain images out there but you needed something that was really awesome and you could not find it on any public domain image site. You can try a stock photography site.

A stock photography website is a place where you can buy professional "stock" images. A stock image is an image taken and sold specifically for distribution. In other words, this is how some professional photographers make their living.

A stock agency usually takes the images on consignment from the photographers and puts them on their website (and possibly others). When the image sells, the photographer gets a royalty from the sale.

These images are not free and sometimes can cost a hundred or more dollars each (unusual) however they are typically the highest quality images and can be very unique. In some cases there are even different pricing models depending on what you want to do with the image. For example there might be one fee for use on a website, and a different fee for publication such as in a book which varies with the number of expected copies of the book.

I suggest you always start with the public domain sources and see if you find something that fits what you need, but when you need the best and you need it now, a stock photography website might be your best solution.

Another nice thing about stock agencies is that they are extremely good about knowing the copyright information and sending you licenses for the use of the image. If you are working on a high profile website and you want to make absolutely sure you have the right to use an image (someone could in theory steal a picture, or buy it from a stock agency and then upload it to a public domain image website) then the stock agency is the way to go.

So where to start with stock agencies? There are three big guys in the business right now: www.istockphoto.com, www.shutterstock.com, and www.gettyimages.com.

The next type of image you may need is a piece of clipart. Clipart is a drawn graphic instead of a photograph which is typically used in logos and letterheads. These are usually vector graphics files meaning that they can be resized to virtually any size without degradation.

You can pick up a variety of free clipart images at www.publicdomainvectors.org.

Let's say you need a logo and can't find one you like for free. Or maybe you need something custom or different. It wasn't that long ago where getting a custom image made was a painful and expensive experience. Now with the worldwide talent pool you can get this done for a really cheap price.

My favorite place for custom artwork is www.fiverr.com. This is an online marketplace where people sell "gigs" typically starting at $5 (plus applicable fees that may add a few cents to the price). Each gig is for a product or service. They usually also offer add-on gigs to extend the service.

Say you want a custom logo made, you pick someone on Fiverr who has a great portfolio and excellent reviews who has a gig where they will create a logo for you for $5 and deliver it in a jpg (nice if you need it one time but not so nice if you want to use the image on your website, business card, and letterhead). Then they offer an add-on gig for $10 where you get the image in its native PSD format (Photoshop). This add-on would allow you to edit the image more if you like and resize it to your heart's content. Total for your image? $5 for the original gig and $10 for the add-on.

Typical add-ons include more or unlimited revisions, the original source file, and delivery of your image faster than normal.

Getting an account on Fiverr.com is free, takes just a few minutes, and makes it easy to get a ton of services you may have never thought of.

A few things to watch for there are that many of the people posting gigs are not from the US and may not speak English as their native language. You can always send them a message and talk to them before buying a gig and can also see the feedback they have left their customers to get a feel for their language skills. Trying to communicate with someone about artwork is hard enough but if their English is horrible it could be an absolute nightmare.

That being said, some of the best and fastest work I have gotten off of there has been from people who did not speak English as their first language. And honestly, some of them from half way around the world spoke better English than some of the people born in the town in Texas where I live, go figure.

Now let's say you need something a little more than what might fit into a gig. This can be up to and including building a huge ecommerce website from scratch to your exacting specifications. It also includes graphic arts, multimedia, writing, sales, marketing, legal, engineering, and much more. Where? www.guru.com.

Guru.com has some pretty good deals although they are typically more expensive than Fiverr.com. Where Guru.com shines is in the higher end landscape. When you need something big, something complex, this is where you go. Heck you could staff a virtual office with people from Guru.com and use them on demand.

5.6 Advertising

There comes a time when you may consider monetizing your website (making money off of it). There are a lot of ways to do this through advertising, more ways than I could reasonably put in this small book, so we are only going to cover a couple to get you started.

This section is more about getting the advertising working on your WordPress website than actually running advertising campaigns. There are a lot of excellent books out there on advertising and marketing so I suggest you get one or more of them to learn about the specifics of advertising.

With that disclaimer out of the way let's talk a little about advertising itself.

Unless you move a large amount of traffic through your website you will not be making enough money to even buy a pizza each month. In fact, if you make enough to buy a soda each month you would be ahead of most of the website operators I know.

In addition, if you put up a bunch of advertising that will actually drive users away so you need to be careful with how much advertising you install while paying particular attention to making sure it is as painless to the user experience as possible.

Advertising works best when it is relevant to the topic of the post or page. What this means is that if you have an excellent post on dieting and weight loss but the ads surrounding this post are for car tires, I would not expect your advertising revenue to be very high. If on the other hand your ads were for dietary supplements and exercise equipment, you might do a little better.

An interesting note is that a small amount of relevant unobtrusive advertising can actually make your website look a little more professional, go figure.

5.6.1 Amazon Associates

The first method of advertising I will be discussing is using Amazon. I really like Amazon for beginners to website advertising as it is very easy to set up, extremely configurable and requires no special software, plugins, or gymnastics to get working well.

We start our journey by visiting affiliate-program.amazon.com where you should see a page similar to this:

Here you can click the Join Now for Free button where it will ask you to enter your Amazon username and password (you do have one of those, right? If not, you can sign up for one now).

Once you have signed up, or signed in and finished your account setup for the Amazon Associates program you should see a page similar to this:

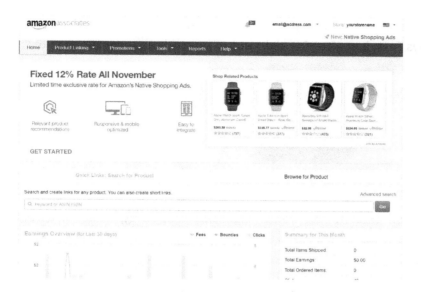

Here you have access to your account, reports, advertisements, and more. There are a lot of features here so spend some time playing around to see what all you can do. Since we are more concerned with getting relevant advertising up in a hurry we will look at getting a single ad up and running for a single product quickly.

Click in your address bar and go to www.amazon.com without logging out of your Amazon Associates account. You should notice this across the top of your browser screen:

This is your SiteStripe and is the tool you use to get advertisements for specific items on Amazon.

Now we need to find an item to advertise and since this is my book, let's do a search for "budget astrophotography" on Amazon and we should see this as our first result (if not, scroll down a little ways to find it).

Click on the title of the book to open its Amazon page and then click on your SiteStripe where it says Text right after Get Link: and you should see something like this:

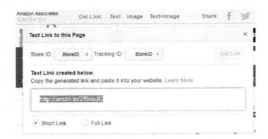

What we are after is that little highlighted piece of code that looks like this: http://amzn.to/2f6voJC. Click in that box and press Ctrl+C on your PC or Command+C on your Mac to copy it to your clipboard.

You can also click the word Image on the SiteStripe to see a screen similar to this:

On this one you can select the size of the image and then copy the highlighted code from the bottom (by using Ctrl+C on your PC or Command+C on your Mac, but not yet, we will do this one in a few minutes).

Now we have both a text and image advertisement we can place on our website so let's do that now.

Open up your WordPress administration screen and go to a post, any post, and edit it. Insert a line of text in the post that says "The best book on budget astrophotography ever written" (I have never had an ego problem, really!). Now highlight the words budget astrophotography that you just typed in by dragging the mouse over them while clicking the left mouse button down until you see something like this:

Click the Link button where the arrow in the previous image is pointing which should bring up this box:

Click in the box where it says Paste URL or type to search and paste the text we have from the Text link above by pressing Crtl+V.

Now you should see the link inserted like above. When anyone clicks the highlighted text it will take them to that item's page and whatever they buy after following that link, you will get a small percentage of. Cool eh?

We used a text link right in the body of a post, you can do the same anywhere there is text such as a page, inside a widget, or a comment. Anywhere you can edit text, you can do the same thing.

Now let's do something a little different by using the Image link instead of the Text link. You can of course do the same thing we just did and have the image appear right in your post, page, or comment but that is too easy. Let's do something a little more interesting and put it in a widget on our sidebar.

Go back to the Amazon page where the item is and click the Image button at the top. Now copy the text at the bottom by pressing Ctrl+C on your PC or Command+C on your Mac.

Open your WordPress administration screen and go to Appearance>Widgets. Drag the Text widget from the left hand side to the bottom of the Sidebar section. When you do it will open up so you can type information in and we will type Advertisement in the Title box followed by pasting in the text we copied into the Content box like this:

Now click Save and go look at the front page of your website, you should see something similar to this:

Text ad

Image ad

Now you can place both kinds of ads virtually anywhere you want on your website. I should mention that you are more than welcome to advertise my books all you want while you are learning about this, or even after.

So why use ads like this targeting a particular item? Often when I am writing a post or page I am telling someone how to do something and they will sometimes need a particular tool or item to be able to complete the task. I can either just tell them what to go get or I can link them directly to what they need to take the guesswork and hassle out of it.

They get exactly the product or tool I am showing them how to use without having to do anything more than click a link, and I get a few cents in the process. Win-win.

Well that is neat and all but there are times when you might want the ads to change or rotate, or maybe I want an ad on a page where there is nothing specific to advertise. Indeed there are ads that are always changing that you can use, let's do that now.

On your SiteStripe click the word SiteStripe to be taken back to the Amazon Associates website (it will open in a new window so you can keep my book in your current window, no pressure).

Now hover the mouse over the Product Linking menu and click on Banners. Under the Promotional Links section click on Easy Links. Scroll down a little until you see the 180 x 150 size and then click in the box with the code which will highlight it like this:

Press your Ctrl+C on your PC or Command+C on your Mac to copy the code to your clipboard and then go to your WordPress administration screen and to Appearance>Widgets. Click the little downward pointing triangle next to the text widget we called Advertisement last time and delete everything out of the Content box. Now click inside that box and press Ctrl+V on the PC or Command+V on the Mac to paste our ad code in it. Click save and go look at your website again.

ADVERTISEMENT

We now have a different ad in the widget on the bottom.

There are way too many types of ads from Amazon Associates to even scratch the surface of what all you can do. There are a ton of different types in many different sizes that do a lot of interesting things so take a look around and play with them. Find ones that work for you and remember to keep the number of ads low so you don't make your users go somewhere else or run an ad blocker so they don't see your ads at all.

5.6.2 Google AdSense

If you do not have a Google account already you can review setting one up in the previous section on Analytics as you will need it here. Once you have a Google account set up you can go to www.google.com/adsense to get started.

Click the Sign In link in the upper right corner and you may see the following box pop up:

> Looks like this Google account isn't associated with an AdSense account. That's okay. You can either sign in with the Google account associated with AdSense, or sign up for an AdSense account today.

Click the Sign Up link in the text and a new screen will appear that asks you if you want to use your current Google login as the login for your AdSense account. Since this is the account we used for Google Analytics I suggest you click the blue Yes button at the bottom.

The next screen asks for your website address which I put in www.ptk4.com and then selected English-English as my content language from the dropdown box. Now click the Save and Continue button.

The next screen asks for your country, time zone, address, phone number, and wants you to select some email preferences (which I always click the box marked No for every one, I have enough spam, thank you). Now click the Submit my application button.

To continue, Google wants to verify your phone number so it presents you with a screen showing your phone number and giving you a choice between receiving a text message or voice call for verification. Typically if you are using a cell phone just select text message as it is easier and faster, otherwise if you entered a landline choose voice call and they will call you and read you a code.

Pick the option you wish to use and click the blue "Send verification code" button. I used a cell phone and had it send me a verification code which was six digits long.

After entering the verification code into the blank provided and clicking the Verify button Google popped up an AdSense Terms and Conditions box which you have to check the checkbox indicating you have read the document (you do read those, right?) and then click the Accept button at the bottom.

Now you get a message thanking you for applying to AdSense and that your account is under review. It also says they will send you an email once your account status changes.

Typically the same day, usually in a few hours, you will get a reply. If you just set up your website and then applied for an AdSense account you will probably be denied with an email like the following:

The reason for this is that Google wants to make sure that you have something they can successfully advertise on. If you have no content, or low quality content, then they don't want to put their advertisements on your site.

In this case I applied with a brand new website and no content at all other than what we have done thus far in this book.

Now what happens if you apply with a website that has plenty of good content (at least I think it's good content!). You get a different email that looks like this:

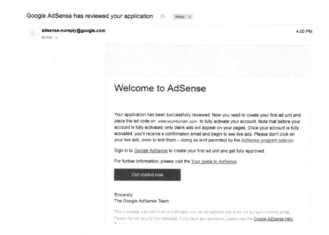

This email is a little different in that they welcome me to AdSense and give me some links to read more about the program. There is also that big blue button near the end of the email that says "Get started now". Let's click the button.

The link in the email takes you to your AdSense page where Google now wants you to verify that you own the website in question.

They do this by asking you to insert a piece of code into the website to they can verify that you have access to it. Click in the box that has the code in it and press Ctrl+C on your PC or Command+C on your Mac to copy the code to your clipboard.

In your WordPress administration screens go to Appearance>Widgets and drag a Text widget over to your sidebar. Now put something in the title (I used AdSense) and then click in the Content box and press Ctrl+V on the PC or Command+V on the Mac to paste the code into the box like this:

Click the blue Save button on the bottom. Now go back to your AdSense page and look near the bottom for the following:

Click in the checkbox and then click the Done button. Now you should see a screen like this one:

Now you sit back and wait while Google looks at your site to find the code. Eventually you should get an email that looks something like this:

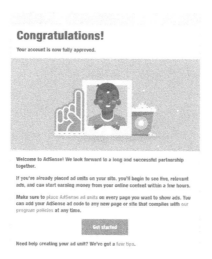

Clicking the Get Started link in the email takes you to your AdSense account page where you should see something like this:

Now we need to set up some ads so click on the Set Up Ads button at the bottom of the page. This takes you to the following screen:

Here we need to click the "New ad unit" button in the upper left of the screen.

On this screen we will fill in a name for the ad, in this case Ad 01, and then click the Save and get code blue button in the lower left. A box should pop up similar to this one:

Clicking in the center box where it says Ad code should highlight all the code in blue at which point you can press Ctrl+C to copy the code to your clipboard.

Now we need a way to place this code into our WordPress website. To start with, we will just put an ad into a text widget. In your WordPress administration screen click on Appearance>Widgets and then drag a Text widget over to your sidebar. (Just like we did to insert the activation code for AdSense, and make sure this one is above the last one we did for AdSense activation).

In the title I suggest you put in Advertisement and then paste your code into the content box below that like this:

Now click the blue Save box at the bottom of the Widget and you should be good to go. It may be a while before you see your first ad so don't panic just yet.

Over to the left of this text is the advertisement we just created dislayed on my website. I set it up in the evening but nothing displayed in the box, the next morning it was showing.

This is the basics of including AdSense on your website. If you want more control over where and how your ads appear there is an excellent plugin called AdSense Integration WP QUADS. To install it simply go to your WordPress administration screen and then Plugins<Add New. Now in the search box in the upper right type in WP QUADS. You should see the following listing:

Click on Install Now and then Activate. Once the plugin is running you will have a new entry in your administration screen's navigation menu called WP QUADS down near the bottom.

This plugin gives you an immense amount of control over what ad goes where. Most of us can get by just fine putting the odd ad in the sidebar or footer widget but when you have a lot of traffic and the potential of significant income from advertising through AdSense this plugin will really let you maximize your income.

If you have more questions about AdSense, there is an entire YouTube channel by Google for AdSense at https://www.youtube.com/playlist?list=PLbAFD4oU9YcpgTcsVPV7cvX2x-YAtdFNY .

5.7 Troubleshooting plugins

Occasionally you will have an issue with a plugin that either just doesn't work correctly or that does not get along with another plugin. When that happens it can be something as minor as some text just does not display as it should or something as major as the entire website no longer works. Time to start troubleshooting plugins.

The first thing you should always do when something does not work correctly is to deactivate the last plugin you activated. You can do that from the plugins page by clicking on the word Deactivate under the plugin name.

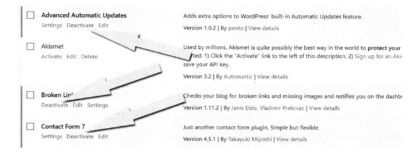

Some plugins may have running processes such as Wordfence and those processes may not stop immediately when you deactivate them. In that case just wait a few minutes after you click the deactivate link and see if your problem disappears.

If deactivating the last plugin you installed does not correct the problem, proceed to the next latest one you installed and deactivate that one, and so on, until the problem is resolved. Just because you installed a plugin yesterday does not mean the one you installed a year ago is not causing the problem. The older one may have just updated, may be clashing with a theme that just updated, etc.

In rare cases it is possible that a plugin keeps the website from working at all. In this case you may not even be able to access the administration screen to deactivate the plugin. If this should happen you will need to either contact the technical support department of your hosting company if you have a managed host such as WordPress.com or you can solve the issue yourself by renaming or deleting the directory that contains the plugin using an FTP program such as FileZilla.

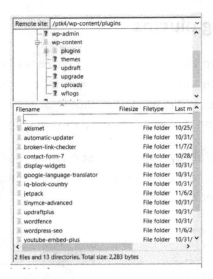

Connect to your website using the instructions found in section 2.2.2 and navigate to the /wp-content/plugins directory as shown above. Note the names of the directories in this location are the same as the names of the plugins. You can download the directory in order to make a backup just in case. Now delete the directory off the server or you can just rename it to something such as renaming the akismet directory to akismet-old.

The next time you attempt to log into your website's administration screen this plugin should no longer be shown.

Just like with the deactivation troubleshooting we did up above if deleting or renaming one of the directories does not work, continue deleting or renaming directories (making sure you have a backup of each one before doing any renaming or deleting) until the problem is resolved.

5.8 The basics of HTML

Knowing the basics of HTML can come in very useful. Not only can it help you understand how things on your site are laid out and how they work, it can also allow you to do some neat things in your pages and widgets.

Basic web pages are typically HTML documents. This is a text file with a .htm or .html extension and can (and use to be) edited in any text editor such as Notepad for Windows or TextEdit for MacOS. What makes these files special is the code used inside.

HTML is made up of tags interspersed with the text displayed on the page. A tag is a command between angle brackets like this:

<COMMAND>

Most tags have an opening tag and a closing tag like this:

<COMMAND> </COMMAND>

Note that the closing tag is just like the opening tag except it has a / before the command. This allows it to tell the web browser that whatever the command is should apply to just the information inside the two tags.

All HTML documents start off with the <HTML> tag at the beginning of the document and end with the </HTML> tag at the end. This tells the web browser that everything in between is considered HTML code.

A great example of what happens with tags around text is the tag to bold text like this:

<B>This text will be bolded</B> and this text will not.

You can also italicize text using the <I></I> tags and underline it using the <U></U> tags.

You may have noticed that all the commands I have typed have been in all upper case and wonder if that is required. No, but it is typically seen as good form when hand writing code. You can use all upper, all lower or any combination. My advice is to pick a method that makes it easier for you to write and read what you have written. Whatever works for you.

Another of my favorite commands for tweaking things is the <CENTER> </CENTER> commands which centers whatever you put in between them.

One command you may find useful is the command to insert an image which looks like this:

<IMG SRC="URL-TO-IMAGE-FILE">

Note that this tag does not have a closing tag. The "URL-TO-IMAGE-FILE" should contain a link to the image you want to display. The following example would display an image of the front cover of one of my books.

<IMG SRC="http://www.allans-stuff.com/wp-content/uploads/2015/09/book-front-300.jpg">

The image tag has some options you can use as well. These options can be defined like this:

<IMG SRC="URL-TO-IMAGE-FILE" ALT="ALTERNATE TEXT" HEIGHT="100" WIDTH="100">

The alt tag is for inputting the alternate text that is read by search engines and screen readers for visually impaired visitors. Height and width can define the absolute height and width the image will be displayed at although I highly discourage using this. It is preferable to resize the image before uploading or using it on the website as it saves space, improves the quality of the resizing, and decreases the time it takes to display the image.

I regularly use the image tag to display images inside text widgets in WordPress and often I combine it with the center tag like this:

<CENTER>

<IMG SRC="http://www.allans-stuff.com/wp-content/uploads/2015/09/book-front-300.jpg">

</CENTER>

This will display the image in the center of the page.

Another useful tag that I use in combination with the image tag (and on its own as well) is the link tag which looks like this:

<A HREF="URL"> </A>

Like most other tags this has an opening and closing tag so that anything in between the two can be clicked on. If you want to combine it with the image tag and center tag we previously used it would look like this:

<CENTER>

<A HREF="http://www.allans-stuff.com/books/bap/">

<IMG SRC="http://www.allans-stuff.com/wp-content/uploads/2015/09/book-front-300.jpg">

</A>

</CENTER>

I have typed these with lines separating them to make them easier to read but the same code works equally well like this:

<CENTER><A HREF="http://www.allans-stuff.com/books/bap/"><IMG SRC="http://www.allans-stuff.com/wp-content/uploads/2015/09/book-front-300.jpg"></A></CENTER>

Other important tags include <BR> which inserts a line break (moves down to the next line) and the <P></P> paragraph tag which defines a paragraph and automatically adds appropriate spacing around it.

5.9 Gravatars

We have talked briefly about Gravatars earlier in the book and now it is time to expand on that a little bit. The name Gravatar comes from the term Globally Recognized Avatar.

All avatars (little pictures beside comments representing the author) in WordPress use Gravatar to display unless you have avatars turned off. In order for this feature to work you must have an account at Gravatar.com and it must use the same email address both on Gravatar.com and when leaving a comment.

The cool thing is that once you have a Gravatar set up, it will show up on all websites that use Gravatars automatically. Let's set one up from scratch and see how it works.

First, go to www.gravatar.com. The first thing you may see at the top looks like this (remember that websites change almost daily so hopefully it is still there and still looks like this):

If you happen to have a WordPress.com account you can log in using your username and password from there. You can also create a WordPress.com account right here to use with Gravatar.

If you don't have a WordPress.com account you can still use Gravatar just fine, look for this button on the Gravatar.com home page instead:

Clicking this button leads to the following screen:

Here you fill out your email address (the one that you will use when posting comments), a username, and a password for this account. Once you are done, the big blue Sign Up button at the bottom will become available so click on it.

You will see a screen that tells you they sent you an email to verify your account. The content of that email may look like this:

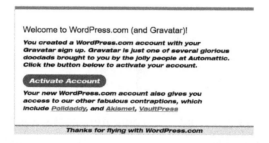

Clicking on the big blue Activate Account button should take you to the WordPress.com website and verify you have been activated by showing this screen:

Now you can click the blue Sign in to Gravatar button to manage your new account.

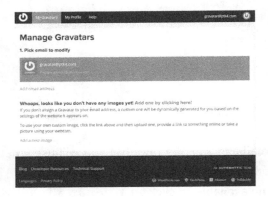

Since we just created this account we only have one email address (you can add more later) and no images. There is a link about center right that says Add one by clicking here! which we will click on now.

Here we can upload our image from our computer, paste the URL of an image already online, look at files we uploaded in the past (which there are none of since this is our first time here), and get an image from our webcam.

Since I already have a picture on my computer I want to use I will work with that first by clicking Upload new in the upper left corner.

Clicking the gray Browse brings up a standard Windows (or MacOS) file dialog box where I can browse my computer to find the file. Once I find it I select it and click the Open button on the bottom of the file dialog box and then the blue Next button you see in the previous image.

Crop your photo using the dotted box below

This screen shows our image and allows us to crop it. Once you are done cropping you can click the blue Crop and Finish button below the image to see this screen:

Choose a rating for your Gravatar

Now we get to choose the rating for our image. Unfortunately since this is user selectable anyone could use any image they want and rate it anything they wanted. I think my image is pretty family safe (although I have had my share of children scream and point at me, aside from around Halloween) so I will select a G rating by clicking on the first box on the left under my picture.

Now we are taken to the following screen:

This completes uploading an image to be our Gravatar but there are still things you can do. Look at the top of the screen and see the My Profile menu item, click on it.

This screen allows you to fill in profile information that can be used by sites and services to let other people know a little about you. There is also a menu over on the right where you can explore a lot more features about your account but that is beyond the scope of this book. Explore, play around, enjoy!

So how do we know it is working? Go to your website and post a comment. I used a different email than my administrator email and made sure I was not logged into the administration screen. Here is the result:

Allan
November 12, 2016 at 5:14 pm

Your comment is awaiting moderation.

Just a test of my gravatar!

Reply

5.10 WordPress file and directory structure

From time to time is it nice to know how files and directories are laid out in a program. You might, for example, need to manually disable a plugin that has stopped your WordPress from loading.

Let's start with extracting the file you downloaded from WordPress.org. When you first extract it you will get a directory called WordPress-4.6.1 (where 4.6.1 is the version you downloaded, it was the current version while I was writing this section of the book). In that directory is another folder called simply WordPress. Looking in that directory will show you this:

```
wp-admin
wp-content
wp-includes
index.php
license.txt
readme.html
wp-activate.php
wp-blog-header.php
wp-comments-post.php
wp-config-sample.php
wp-cron.php
wp-links-opml.php
wp-load.php
wp-login.php
wp-mail.php
wp-settings.php
wp-signup.php
wp-trackback.php
xmlrpc.php
```

This is called the WordPress root directory and typically should be in the root directory of your web server. You could also have a traditional website and put this in a subdirectory of your website such as www.yourdomain.com/blog. This would allow you to run your WordPress as a component of your existing website which I had done several years ago.

A common mistake is that people extract the WordPress-4.6.1 file and then upload the WordPress folder that is inside it to their root website directory. This puts their WordPress installation in www.yourdomain.com/WordPress which is not what they really wanted.

The files in this root directory are the files that are responsible for WordPress being able to connect to the database (where all the information such as option, users, posts, pages, and comments are stored) as well as connect the website visitor to WordPress.

You are already familiar with the wp-config.php file as this is where we entered the information such as database name, user name, and password that connected your WordPress website to its database. What you may not know is there are many other configuration options you can enter into this file to change the way WordPress behaves.

While there are far too many options for me to cover here you can find all the options available at https://codex.WordPress.org/Editing%20wp-config.php. Let's look at a couple of things you can do just so you get a feel for them.

You can force all user logins to the administration screen to use SSL (connect using https: instead of just http:) by inserting the following line in the wp-config.php file.

```
define( 'FORCE_SSL_ADMIN', true );
```

There are several other things that must be working before you turn on SSL logins which you can read about at https://codex.WordPress.org/Administration_Over_SSL.

You can move the wp-content folder to a different location by using this line:

```
define( 'WP_CONTENT_DIR', dirname( __FILE__ ) . '/blog/wp-content' );
```

When editing the wp-config.php file make sure you do not add, edit, or remove anything below the following line:

```
/* That's all, stop editing! Happy blogging. */
```

The file that loads and starts the website visitor's experience is the index.php file. If this file is missing you would get an error and your site would not load. Another common issue is that you do not delete all the files on your server before uploading the WordPress installation and so there are several files in the root directory that all try to do the same thing.

Files with names such as default.htm, default.html, index.htm, index.html, and index.php all do the same job and it is up to the web server configuration as to what order they are looked for and loaded.

If you happen to have an index.htm from an old website beside the new index.php from WordPress and the web server is set to load index.htm before index.php then your website will continue to function even after uploading WordPress.

Since the web server's configuration is probably not something you have access to the solution is to remove or rename the index.htm document. I usually recommend deleting the entire old website, complete with all the files and directories before WordPress installation to help prevent this problem (after making a backup of course).

If you need to retain the original index.htm file but do not want it to load, simply rename the file to index.ht1 or index.old. I personally like the index.ht1 as it allows me to make up to nine backups of a file which does happen sometimes.

There are three directories in this root directory. Two of these are wp-admin and wp-includes which represent the actual WordPress program files called the core. For 99% of the WordPress users out there, these folders should never be touched. Virtually anything you do inside them will cause things to break. Leave them alone.

The third directory inside the root directory is the wp-content directory. This is where all uploaded files, plugins, and themes are kept. A new install of WordPress, or the WordPress archive downloaded from WordPress.org will contain the following:

plugins
themes
index.php

Note that there is no uploads folder. This will be created by WordPress once you actually upload a file.

If we look inside the plugins directory we might see something like this:

akismet
automatic-updater
auto-terms-of-service-and-privacy-policy
broken-link-checker
contact-form-7
jetpack
hello.php
index.php

Here we see a folder for each plugin we have installed. If we installed akismet and then our website would no longer work we might want to disable that plugin. But if we cannot get to the website to log in and get to our plugins screen, how do we disable the plugin?

Simply use an FTP program (like the FileZilla program we used earlier in this book) to delete the akismet directory inside the plugins directory and you should be able to log back in to your website.

The same holds true of the themes directory although I have not seen where a theme could completely disable a website to the point where you could not log into the administration screen.

Once you upload some files to WordPress and it creates the uploads directory it will keep files in the following structure:

root\wp-content\uploads\2015\09

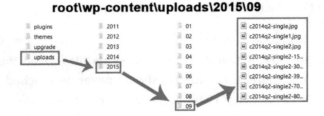

If you started your website in 2016, everything you uploaded to your media library would be inside the 2016 directory and then inside another folder with the number of the month you uploaded that file. In the example shown above, those images on the far right side were uploaded into that WordPress website in September of 2015.

As you look around you may find other files and folders than the ones we have talked about. For example in the previous image there is a directory in the wp-content directory called upgrade which is a folder used by the upgrade feature inside WordPress.

The Updraft plugin also likes to put a folder inside the wp-content directory in addition to the one it puts in the plugins directory.

Hopefully this gives you enough of a working knowledge of the structure of the WordPress file system to help you should you need it.

Section 6: Going even further

Congratulations! You have completed the book and should be well on your way to having a website you can be proud of.

Just because the book is over does not mean the learning is. There is no way anyone could ever hope to include everything there is to know about WordPress in one book. Not only that but there are things such as HTML and PHP that, while not typically considered a part of WordPress, is what WordPress is built on and can certainly help you extend its functionality even further.

To that end I am including a wealth of information in the back of this book on where you can go from here, as well as a glossary and index to make sure you get the most out of the information you already have.

Lastly, I will include information on a few book titles I wrote that you may be interested in.

I hope you enjoyed the book and learned a lot from it. If so, please take a minute to leave the book a review on Amazon.com. If you found a problem, have a concern or did not like it for some reason please stop by my website at www.allans-stuff.com and use the contact form to leave me a message. I genuinely want to make this the best book I can so your feedback is very important to me.

6.1 Where to go from here

Now that you have the basics down, where can you go to learn more?

Books

WordPress: The Missing Manual 2nd Edition by Matthew MacDonald

Professional WordPress: Design and Development by Brad Williams, David Damstra, and Hal Stern

WordPress Web Application Development by Rakhitha Nimesh Ratnayake

HTML: QuickStart Guide - The Simplified Beginner's Guide To HTML (HTML, HTML5, HTML and CSS) by ClydeBank Technology and Martin Mihajlov

PHP: Learn PHP in 24 Hours or Less by Robert Dwight (Author)

Websites

www.WordPress.org – The home of all things WordPress including the program, codex (documentation), support forums, plugins directory and themes directory.

www.welovewp.com - Theme and inspiration gallery which is sure to give you ideas on how to make your website awesome.

www.wpbeginner.com – Great place for information and video tutorials on the fundamentals of WordPress.

Gatherings

www.wordcamp.org – Find camps around the world focused on all levels of WordPress users, developers, and more.

6.2 Index

6.3 Glossary

Administration Screen – The screens and menus you log into and use in order to create and manage a WordPress website. When you first log in the administration screen presents the Dashboard in the work area which is the large area on the right, a toolbar across the top and a navigation menu with menu items on a strip down the left hand side. As a whole, this is the administration screen.

Administrator – The person who owns or is the primary operator of a WordPress website. This person has the highest security access to all areas of the installation and cannot be demoted by any other non-administrator users.

Alt Text – A description applied to a media item such as an image that search engines and people with visual (in the case of images and videos) or hearing (in the case of audio files) impairments use to know what the media is supposed to represent. In the case of the visually impaired this text is often read to them by their screen reading software.

App – A small program that runs on a device such as a smartphone or tablet, or on a desktop operating system such as Windows or MacOS and acts as a front end for a website. This usually makes for a better experience than using a web browser and may be slightly faster but can also have limitations as the website often has more functionality and scalability. Apps almost always require an internet connection to function. Examples include the Facebook and Twitter apps.

Application – A program usually installed on a desktop or laptop computer that has complete functionality without being required to connect to the internet. They may however require internet access to activate or install, but not to run. Examples include Intuit's QuickBooks, Adobe's Photoshop, and Microsoft's Word.

Article – A page, post, or comment. Anything that can combine text, images, audio, and video into a single unified display for the visitor. Think of it as a newspaper or magazine article which can be displayed in several different manners.

Author (post/page/comment) – The person who wrote a post, page, or comment. There can be several authors who can all work on a single post or page and they are all considered authors.

Author (role) – Someone who can write posts without waiting for approval and manage the ones that they wrote but not the posts of other people.

Avatar – A small graphical representation or picture of a user. These are typically used in comments and in the upper right corner of the WordPress administration screen to show who is currently logged in.

Background – Refers to an image that is placed behind all other items on a page such as text and media. The background may be applied to the entire page or only a section.

Best Practices – Ways and methods of doing things that are accepted as the best way to do them by a large percentage of people. For example it is a best practice to always look both ways before crossing a road.

Blacklist – A list used to deny access to something. An example in WordPress is if a word is on the blacklist in Settings>Discussion, any comment that contains that word will be placed in the trash immediately.

Blockquote – A section of text that is highlighted in such a way to make it obvious that you are quoting another source. This section is usually in a highlighted rectangle, hence the term block. The appearance of the block is dictated by the theme and can differ greatly from theme to theme. Some themes allow for customizing the block.

BLOG – Short for weB LOG. Much like a diary or journal posted online instead of written in a book. Blogs are what WordPress was originally designed to provide.

Bot – A computer program that automatically visits websites. These bots can be used to retrieve data, attempt logins, probe for security vulnerabilities, and check for copyright violations among many other tasks.

Browser – See Web Browser.

CAPTCHA - Completely Automated Public Turing test to tell Computers and Humans Apart. A system by where a test is performed with the intent of making sure the respondent is human and not a computer program. This is useful in reducing spam comments and contact form submissions.

Caption – A portion of text that appears underneath an image on a page or post. This text is usually used to describe the image so that it makes more sense to the reader. It should be rarely used as the image used should not be so obscure as to require a caption.

Cascading Style Sheet – A method of keeping the display configuration (fonts, colors, styles) in a separate file from the base HTML documents. This allows many HTML pages to all draw from one CSS page so that if you wanted to change the style of all the pages at once you only had one place to make that change.

Category – A method of dividing posts into sections or containers to make them easier to navigate. A visitor to your site could then browse posts within a specific category instead of having to look through all posts including ones they were not interested in.

Child – A child object (menu item, page, category, etc.) is an object underneath another object called the parent in a hierarchal organization structure. An example might be a parent organization called cars could have a child of sedan which in turn could be the parent of a child called four door. A child must have a parent but a parent need not have a child.

Chrome – A free web browser created by Google known for its speed and low memory usage. Chrome is available for Windows, MacOS, Linux, and Android.

CMS – See Content Management System.

Code – The text that is not shown to the visitor and controls placement, formatting, and other attributes of the items on the page. Code in WordPress is usually in HTML or PHP languages.

Codex – The official WordPress documentation available online at www.WordPress.org.

Comment – A reply to a post, page or other comment made by a visitor to the website. It is typically used to allow for discussion about the post or page it was posted to.

Content Management System – A program such as WordPress that is used to make creating, editing, and displaying content such as text, images, and videos easier. Typically these systems allow for multiple people to work on the system simultaneously and in collaboration with one another.

Contribute – A program created by Adobe to create and manage websites. Contribute, as its name implies, allows multiple people to work in a network type environment and contribute to the website as a whole. Much of the need for such software has been eliminated by software such as WordPress.

Contributor – A role within WordPress where the user can create and edit their own posts but have to have their posts approved before they are published.

CSS – See Cascading Style Sheet.

Dashboard – The initially displayed screen when you log into the administration area of a WordPress website. This configurable screen displays a wealth of information from different plugins and parts of WordPress in a central location.

Database – A method or program to store data in such a way that it can be indexed and retrieved quickly. Databases are generally highly scalable and can store vast quantities of data while still retrieving search results very quickly. WordPress uses the MySQL database as its default back data storage medium.

Dedicated Hosting – A plan from a web hosting company whereby your website is hosted on its own server or virtual server (for virtual dedicated hosting). This typically provides more power and speed than other types of hosting which allows you to service more users faster. It is typically the most expensive option web hosting companies offer and is reserved for the largest and busiest of websites.

Device – Typically refers to a smartphone or tablet but can also mean any electronic item that has computing power and can run apps other than traditional computers. Today devices can include television sets, game consoles, and even refrigerators.

Discussion – Refers to a conversation about a topic using posts and comments to continue dialog and get users participating. This increases interest and can drive more traffic to your site.

DNS – See Domain Name System.

Domain Name – For the purposes of this book it is the name of your website. Examples include yahoo.com, amazon.com, and ebay.com. These names are bought per year from a registrar such as godaddy.com.

Domain Name System – A hierarchical system of naming devices connected to the internet managed by ICANN which is then translated into the actual numerical Internet Protocol (IP) addresses on which the internet uses to function.

Download – Transferring a file or files from somewhere on the internet to your computer or device is called downloading.

Draft – A saved document that has not been sent or published so that you can continue to work on it at a later time until you are ready to send or publish it. This term is common to both email and WordPress.

Dropdown – Refers to a menu that appears to open up when you click on it and has several items in a list that you can choose from. Typical dropdown boxes allow for a single selection although some do offer the ability to select multiple items.

Edge – A web browser written by Microsoft and introduced in Windows 10 as a replacement to the Internet Explorer web browser included in prior versions of Windows. Edge is a completely new program and not a new version of Internet Explorer. While faster and more secure than Internet Explorer it has some issues with interactive website and just recently gained the ability to use extensions. Microsoft has stated they will only be working on Edge from now on instead of releasing new versions of Internet Explorer.

Editor – A facility to make changes to items in WordPress. The editor for posts, pages, and comments is the TinyMCE editor and there is a separate editor for working with code sections such as in themes and plugins.

Editor (role) – A user that can not only write, edit, and publish their own posts but also has the ability to edit and publish the posts of other people such as authors, contributors and subscribers.

EMD – See Exact Match Domain.

Exact Match Domain – A domain name that is an exact match for a term or phrase a typical visitor might use in a search engine. For example, stuntkites.com would be an EMD for people searching for stunt kites.

Export – A function where all the text and links in a WordPress website can be downloaded in a single file. Useful for backups and for use in moving a website from one domain to another either on the same server or a different server.

Expression Web – A program from Microsoft for designing and maintaining websites. Expression Web was discontinued in 2012 and is available for free online at microsoft.com/expression.

Extensible Markup Language – Commonly known as XML this is a language similar to HTML in look and feel that is meant to be readable by both people and computers. It is also a self-descriptive language in that everything needed to decode what is inside the document is inside that document. It is commonly used to transfer data between dissimilar software or hardware platforms.

Feed – A regularly updated listing of the most recent posts on a website distributed in such a format that "feed readers" or "feed aggregators" can retrieve the feed from the website and post that information on a different website. As new posts are made, they are added to the top of the feed while the older ones falls off the bottom. The feed aggregator then notices the change in the feed and grabs the new post for its readers.

Feedback – A message generally sent from a visitor to the administrator of a website letting them know what they think. This can be done via comments or a contact form among other ways. Common uses are to report errors or problems.

File Transfer Protocol – A method of transferring files between computers. Typically used to transfer files to and from a computer locally to one on the internet. This was once the only way to work with files on a website as you would edit them on your local computer and then FTP them (upload them via FTP) to your web server. The most common FTP program in use today is FileZilla.

FileZilla – A free open source program for performing file transfers using the FTP protocol. FileZilla is available from filezilla-project.org.

Filter – A method of restricting the display of items to only those that match a specific criteria. You could for example filter a list of themes to only those that contain the color red.

Firefox – A free open source web browser very popular in the tech community. Firefox is available for Windows, MacOS, Linux, and Android. You can download Firefox from www.mozilla.org.

Fly-Out – A type of menu or item that when a mouse is hovered over, or clicked to select an item, another item or menu appears to slide out from, fly out from, or appear beside/below/above the original item. This is a common way to employ nested menus as when one menu item is clicked additional choices are presented to refine the visitor's section.

Footer – The area at the bottom of a web page stretching horizontally across the page.

Form – A screen or page with areas where you can type information in and/or select from predefined data sets. Forms are often used as login screens, means of sending contact information, and finding information on a website.

Format (posts) – A method some themes use to change the way a post is displayed to the visitor in WordPress depending on the type of content or intended use of the post. WordPress includes several different formats by default although not that many themes make use of them.

Forum – A special type of website designed primarily for people to communicate with each other by making a post and replying to those posts. Unlike regular websites or blogs, there is not one person or group creating the content but all of the users of the forum instead. Forums are typically devoted to a specific theme or topic such as a particular car, piece of software, or hobby.

Front Page – The first page a visitor to your website sees.

FTP – See File Transfer Protocol.

Function (code) – A particular piece of code that is run when that particular functionality is required. For example your program could have a function that when someone enters a number and then presses the * key followed by another number, those two numbers would be multiplied together. Functions can be written once and then used anywhere else in the program without having to rewrite the code.

Gears (Google) – A toolkit developed by Google that extended the capabilities of HTML code to make for faster processing, offline data use, and other features. Most of the functionality was eventually included into HTML 5 making it no longer required and so it was discontinued in late 2011.

Grayed Out – A menu item, selector, or other object is said to be grayed out when its colors are either subdued or desaturated and it does not function. Items are typically grayed out because that function is not available due to missing information or because that function would not be applicable at this time.

Hacker – A person who causes something to happen by a means that was unintended. Hackers are typically portrayed as nefarious individuals however hacking can be either good or bad depending on the use. For the purposes of this book a hacker is someone you want to avoid.

Header – The very top portion of a website running horizontally across the page. Headers are very common but are not necessarily included in all themes.

Hierarchy – A method of classification and storage that uses a parent child relationship between members. Using kites as an example the top of the hierarchy could be kites which is the parent of the child single line kites and dual line kites. Each of these two could be the parents of their own children in turn. The way files and folders work on most modern operating systems is an example of an hierarchal storage system.

Hijack – The act of taking something over in part or in totality. For this book hijacking is meant to convey that someone will take partial or total control of your website and use it for their own uses. This could be something as simple as displaying an ad or link that you did not know of or it could completely replace your website and deny you access.

Home Page – See Front Page.

Hosting – The act of putting a website on a server in such a way as to allow people on the internet to view and interact with it.

Hosting Service – A company that provides the servers, internet connection, and facilities to host your website on the internet.

HTML – See Hyper Text Markup Language.

Hyper Text Markup Language – A programming language that is the basis for all web pages.

ICANN – See Internet Corporation for Assigned Names and Numbers.

Icon – A very small graphical image used to represent something. Typical uses for icons include for programs, websites, and files.

Import – The ability for WordPress to load a single file that was exported from a WordPress website that contains all the text from posts, pages, and comments and recreate those items. This is typically done in order to move a website from one domain to another, from one hosting company to another, or as a crude way of backing up and restoring data after a crash.

Installer – A program or piece of code that installs something. Installers are used in WordPress as well as with most computer programs today. Once the installation of the program or code is complete the installer ceases to run and is not used again unless the program or code needs to be uninstalled or reinstalled.

Interface – The part of a program or website that a person interacts with. WordPress has an interface for the administrator, WordPress.com has their own simplified interface for WordPress and the website is yet another interface except it is designed for the visitor.

Internet Corporation for Assigned Names and Numbers – The organization that is over all domain name issuance, management, and records for the entire internet. Domain name registrars all report to and derive their authority to sell you a domain name from ICANN.

Internet Explorer – A web browser built by Microsoft that has been included with every version of Windows since Windows 95. Internet Explorer is the most widely distributed web browser as it is included on every Windows based computer shipped. With Windows 10 Microsoft has included Edge which is their replacement for Internet Explorer. The last version of Internet Explorer is 11.

Java – A programming language often used in web design that can run on Windows, MacOS, Linux, Android, and iOS as well as others. Java allows web developers to produce rich interactive applications online with a write-once run-everywhere platform.

Keyword – A word used to help visitors find specific content on your website. Keywords can be assigned to posts and the visitor can search for those keywords to find posts they are interested in.

Library – A collection of items. Your media library in WordPress is a collection of all the media (images, audio, and video files) that you have uploaded to your website.

Linux – A free open source operating system similar in functionality to Microsoft's Windows and Apple's MacOS popular in the tech community. Linux can offer the user most of the functionality of traditional operating systems with only a slightly higher technical knowledge requirement.

Log In/Login – Entering a username and password to gain access to a restricted portion of a website. You log in to your WordPress administration screen.

Macintosh – A computer platform built by Apple. Commonly referred to as Macs and running the MacOS these computers are popular with content creators such as website designers, graphic artists, writers, video editors, and photographers. Typically more expensive but more stable and less likely to be infected by spyware/viruses, these computers represent approximately 5% of the online computers today.

MacOS – The operating system developed by Apple for their Macintosh computers.

Mail Server – A computer connected to the internet whose job it is to send, receive, and route email. These are the computers whose addresses you put in your email program's configuration or that you connect to when you go to webmail such as gmail.com.

Managed Hosting – A service provided by a hosting company where they take care of the general maintenance of your WordPress installation such as installation, general configuration, updates, and backups. These plans often include WordPress specific technical support and generally cost slightly more than non-managed plans.

Media – Refers to non-text items used in a website including images, audio, and video.

Menu – An area or device that contains things the user can interact with in order to navigate around the website. Examples include a bar with words on it and as you click on one of the words that causes you to be taken to a different area of the website.

Migration – The act of moving from one to another. Examples include moving from one hosting company to another can be said to migrate from one hosting company to another. Migration can be done automatically through a program or service or manually.

Mobile – When browsing a website from a device that is not connected using any cables that device is said to be mobile. Mobile devices typically include smartphones and tablets but may also include infotainment systems in vehicles.

Moderation – A comment may be held for moderation meaning that it is not posted where any typical website visitor can see it until an administrator or someone with moderation rights can read the comment and approve it, at which time it is removed from the moderation queue and posted publicly. This is used as a method to control spam and inappropriate behavior.

MySQL – A database program by Oracle that has both a commercial version and a freely available community version. MySQL is extremely popular on the internet and specifically for websites such as those run on WordPress.

Nested (menus) – Refers to a menu where a main topic is displayed and when that topic is hovered over or clicked more menu items appear to refine the selection. An example might be on www.allans-stuff.com there is a menu item called "My Books" that when you hover over it a list of all the books I have written appears below the menu. You can then click on the title of the book you are interested in to go to that book's page.

Notification – A term used to describe a method of communicating to the administrator of a website that something has happened. This can be by sending the administrator an email or displaying an indicator on the administration screen. These can include such things as telling the administrator that there are updates available, comments have been made, or an administrator has logged into the system.

Open Source – A piece of software or program that is worked on by a community of people potentially from all over the world which is typically provided for free for anyone to modify and use. Called open source because the source code (the actual programming that makes it work) is freely available for anyone to read, modify, and use in their own projects.

Operating System – The program that is used to make your computer functional. Typical operating systems include Microsoft Windows, Apple MacOS and Linux for desktop computers and Android and iOS for devices such as smartphones and tablets.

OS – See Operating System.

Package – An offering from a hosting company which typically includes several services bundled together into a single "package" for a set price per month or year. Different packages will have different options and different prices.

Page (website) – Generally a single file of information (although it can be multiple files in more complex websites) that is displayed to the website visitor as a single screen.

Page (WordPress) – A type of article that is usually not updated frequently and tends to display static information to the visitors. Examples of page titles would be About Us, Contact Us, Sales Information and Downloads.

Parent – In a parent-child relationship the parent is the primary while the child is secondary. An example might be the General Motors is the parent to Chevrolet while Chevrolet is the parent to the Malibu car.

Permalink – A URL or link to a post, page, or other resource on a website that is meant to remain unchanged for long periods of time such as years. This is a common term used with posts as the post will typically move down the page on the website as new posts are written however the permalink will always remain the same no matter how many posts are written or how far down the page the post that the permalink points to moves.

Phone – Refers to a smartphone or smart cell phone.

PHP – A server-side (runs on the server) scripted (as compared to a compiled language) programming language that can be embedded in HTML code or run as standalone files. PHP is very common on the web, extensively used throughout WordPress, its themes, and its plugins. It is also extremely popular for interfacing web pages with database servers.

Ping – See Pingback.

Pingback – A system where when you link to a post on another website that has pingback enabled the author of that post will receive a pingback notification that you have linked to his post. If you have pingbacks enabled then you will receive notification if someone on another site links to your post in their post, assuming they also have pingbacks enabled.

Plan – See Package.

Platform – A basic style of hardware such as a tablet, phone, or desktop computer monitor. The platform has nothing to do with the operating system running on a device and only generally with the size. A big enough difference in size could be termed a different platform such as going from a small 6" tablet to a 12" or larger tablet. Even though the operating system, style, manufacturer, and interface may be identical between those two sizes there is enough difference in size that the interface might need to be substantially different for them to work well and hence they be considered a different platform.

Plugin – A piece of code or software that can be installed in WordPress to extend or change the functionality of the core WordPress program. Examples of popular plugins include automated backups, language translators, and security programs.

Post – A type of article on a WordPress website that is typically used for a new or blog article. These are typified by being displayed in chronological order from newest to oldest.

Preview – Allows you to see what a post or page will look like to a visitor.

Profile – A collection of information about a user or visitor which can include things such as name, email address, webpage, password and biographical information.

Program – A piece of software which contains instructions telling the computer what to do when certain things happen, usually due to input from a user. Programs can be as simple as a calculator or as complex as a full accounting package like QuickBooks.

Programming Language – A written language designed to allow a person writing that language to tell a computer what to do.

Radio Button – A small round symbol that when clicked indicates it is selected by putting a small black dot in the middle. Radio buttons can allow only one selection per group or multiple selections per group.

Readability – A general measurement of how easy it is for someone to read the text in a page or post. Text should be easy to read without talking down to the visitor. Easy to read posts and pages are generally ranked higher by search engines.

reCAPTCHA – Google's version of a CAPTCHA which has a wide following and is continually updated. Free for anyone to use and built into plugins such as Contact Form 7, you can sign up for an account at google.com/recaptcha.

Registrar – A company whose job it is to register domain names with ICANN on your behalf. You pay them a yearly fee for registration of a domain name and they in turn make sure the primary domain name servers around the world recognize that name and point visitors in the right direction.

Role – The security classification of a user in WordPress. There are multiple roles in WordPress that allow different actions or permissions. A user can be assigned to only one role at a time.

Safari – A web browser developed by Apple that comes standard on all Apple computers and devices. Overall a very stable and capable browser on all platforms however Apple keeps pretty strict rules in place making it less expandable than other browsers on the same operating systems. Safari is available only for Apple operating systems although it was available for Windows from 2007 through 2012.

Scalable – The ability of an item to provide more resources as the demand for those resources increases. When talking about web hosts for example, as the number of visitors to a website increases it takes more CPU, memory, and hard drive access to keep up with that demand. If the web host is highly scalable that means they will not have a problem providing increased CPU, memory, and hard drive access to keep up with that demand.

Screenshot – An image of a computer screen typically used to illustrate or teach computer related topics.

Search Engine Optimization – The act of altering the content or layout of a page, post, or entire website so that search engines will show results from that website higher in search results than they would without such optimizations.

Second Level Domain – The portion of a domain name just before the Top Level Domain. In Yahoo.com the "Yahoo" portion is the second level domain.

Security – Ensuring that only those persons or actions that are intended and allowed to perform an action are actually the only ones that can perform that action.

SEO – See Search Engine Optimization.

Server – A computer whose job it is to hand out, or serve, data to other computers. Servers are usually more powerful computers than the typical home computer and in the case of the internet stored in large data centers where there may be hundreds of servers all working together. Typical uses for servers include hosting websites, providing email services, storing data and processing transactions.

Shared Hosting – Where more than one website is installed and running on a single server computer thereby sharing the resources of that server between all the websites that are running on it. Shared hosting is the least expensive method of providing web hosting and virtually all of the plans being used by individuals and small businesses are shared hosting plans.

Sharing – Refers to the ability of visitors to post information on their social networking sites such as Facebook and Twitter about your website. Usually done through buttons that allow them to "share" your posts with their friends on that social networking site.

Shortcode – A small piece of code, usually less than fifty or so characters, which allows you to insert something into a page or post in WordPress. Shortcodes such as [Best_WordPress_Gallery id="21" gal_title="Caldwell-DSLR"] can insert an entire photo gallery into a page or post containing over a hundred images.

Sidebar – The area on a WordPress website where widgets can be placed. There can be one or more depending on the themes. This is another name for widgetized area.

SLD – See Second Level Domain.

Social – Refers to social networking sites such as Facebook and Twitter.

Spam – Refers to unwanted comments, replies, links, posts, emails, or contact form submissions. Generally used as a form of advertising or promotion of another website without your permission.

Spider – A spider is an automated computer program that visits websites typically to index pages (make information you have on your website appear in search engines). All of the major search engines employ spiders including Google, Yahoo, and Bing.

Static (page) – A page that does not change and is therefore static.

Sticky – A post that remains at the top regardless of the date it was posted or the number of posts made before or after it was published. Normally posts move down the page as a new post is made however making a post sticky forces it to be the one at the top forever. This is useful for making sure something (such as rules, a readme, or important information) is always at the top for every visitor.

Sub-Menu – A menu or set of options that usually appears below and slightly off to the right of a menu or menu item. This below and right display is meant to denote that these are options for the main menu item.

Subdomain – The left most portion of a domain name which is used to route traffic to specific services or portions of a website. Most popular with websites would be the www subdomain but you may have also seen ftp and mail as subdomains.

Subscriber – The lowest security level of roles in WordPress who can only manage their own profile and can not write or manage posts at all.

Tab – Usually found at the top of a page, a tab is an organizational section marker like a manila folder tab in that it denotes a section that can be viewed by clicking that tab. Clicking on a tab displays a page related to that tab's subject while clicking a different tab displays a different page related to that tab's subject.

Tablet – A handheld touchscreen computer usually running Android or iOS (or Windows in the case of a Microsoft Surface tablet) designed to be used primarily without a mouse, keyboard, or external monitor. Tablets usually have less power, memory, and storage than a traditional computer but are substantially more portable. Tablets are generally too large to be used as a phone comfortably.

Tag (WordPress) – A keyword used to help a user find a post. Tags are usually defined as or after a post is written and helps narrow a search more than a category would. An example might be a post about kites and the category might be stunt kites while the tags might include box (the type of kite), rayon (the material the kite is made from) and red (the color of the kite).

Tag (HTML) – A command used in HTML.

Theme – A set of files that define the overall look and feel of a WordPress website as well as placement for menus, widgets, headers, footers, and other structural elements. Themes can be free or paid for and can either be installed using the built in installer or uploaded from your computer. There are thousands of themes currently available.

Thumbnail – A small version of an image that is meant to be a representation of that image.

Tiled – When an image is too small to take up the entire screen (or area it is assigned to) then that image can be repeated over and over again just like the tiles you use in a bathroom or kitchen floor.

TinyMCE – The name of the default editor for posts and pages in WordPress.

TLD – See Top Level Domain.

Toolbar – An area running across the top of the web browser with menu options allowing for access to certain controls of WordPress. This bar is visible once you log into your WordPress website when you are in the administration screen or viewing the website.

Top Level Domain – The portion of a domain name on the very end after the last ".". Popular TLDs include .com, .net, and .org although there are many others.

Uniform Resource Locator – The address of an object on the internet, typically thought to be a website address such as http://www.allans-stuff.com but can also be other services such as ftp:// or mail:// or file://.

Update – As programs, themes, and plugins are found to have flaws or their authors decide to add new functionality, they may release a new version of the software. These new versions are called updates and are displayed in the update area of the WordPress administration screen. You are only notified of updates to items you have currently installed.

Upload – Transferring a file from your local computer over the internet to your WordPress website is called uploading a file.

URL – See Uniform Resource Locator.

Users – A section in the WordPress navigation menu where you can view, edit and change information regarding website visitors who have registered in WordPress. This includes you as the administrator.

Version – A version of a piece of software is analogous to the year model of a car. When new versions are released they typically fix problems with the old version and possibly add new functionality. Unlike year models of cars, free plugins and themes are updated without cost. If you have a paid plugin or theme you may have to pay an upgrade fee.

Virtual Hosting – A method of hosting a website where each website on a shared server has a specific amount of access to the CPU, memory, and hard drive as if it was on a computer all by itself. When the website attempts to exceed these limits, instead of taking resources away from other websites on the same physical server, it is denied access to any more resources and is made to do with what it has. This makes sure that no one website can slow down the others on the same physical computer. Virtual hosting is generally more expensive than shared hosting but substantially cheaper than dedicated hosting.

Virtual Machine – One physical computer can have its resources divided into several virtual computers. If for example one computer were divided into four virtual machines each of those virtual machines would have access to only 25% of the available hard drive space and could not exceed that. The virtual machine is what runs the virtual web host.

Visitor – A person who uses a web browser to look at your web site or a computer program that reads the data from your website such as a bot or spider.

Web Browser – A program designed to read the various languages of code (HTML, PHP, JavaScript) sent out by a web server and display a web page for the visitor and allow them to interact with it. Web browsers are installed on the visitor's computer or device. Popular web browsers include Edge, Internet Explorer, Safari, Chrome, and Firefox.

Web Host - A company that provides servers and facilities where your website can be connected to the internet. Professional web hosting companies typically have multiple levels of redundancy, backup generators, and technical staff on site at all times.

Website – A collection of information which can include text, images, audio, video, and other files that are presented in a cohesive way to people visiting that site with a web browser.

What You See Is What You Get – A type of page or post editor where instead of working with code that does not represent the final product, as you type or insert media you see exactly what the visitor will see as you build the page or post.

Widget – A small application in WordPress that performs a specific function in an area of the site called a widget area set aside specifically for widgets.

Widget Area – An area on a WordPress website denoted by the active theme that allows the placement of widgets. A particular theme may allow widgets on one or multiple areas. Typical areas for widgets include one or more sidebars and near or in the footer.

Windows – An operating system by Microsoft that runs on Intel compatible hardware. Windows is the most popular operating system in use on desktop and laptop computers today.

WordPress – A free open source program designed to make the creation, updating, and installation of an interactive website easy and fast. It is also the subject of this book!

WordPress.com – A website that specializes in providing hosting solutions, including free packages, to people wanting to run the WordPress software provided by WordPress.org.

WordPress.org – The website run by the developers and supporters of WordPress. This is where you can download the software, themes, plugins, read the documentation, and get support from the community.

WYSIWYG – See What You See Is What You Get.

XML – See Extensible Markup Language.

Zip – A type of file compression that allows for one or many files to be put inside a single compressed file that can be substantially smaller than the sum of the original file(s). This allows for faster uploads and downloads, keeping multiple related files together, and prevents alteration of the files as they cannot be altered while inside a compressed state.

Zipped – An item that has been compressed using zip compression.

6.4 More titles by this author

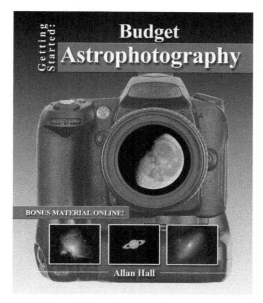

Want to take a few snapshots of the beautiful objects you are viewing without spending a small fortune? Already have a camera but you can't seem to get a good image and want to know why?

This book will answer those and many other questions while giving you a quick and reasonably easy introduction to budget astrophotography. In addition, save more money by learning how to make a lot of items you may find useful.

http://www.allans-stuff.com/bap/

If you decide that you want more than quick snapshots, you want big beautiful prints to hang on your wall, this is the book for you.

From required and optional equipment, through the capture process and into the software processing needed to create outstanding images, this book will walk you through it all.

http://www.allans-stuff.com/leap/

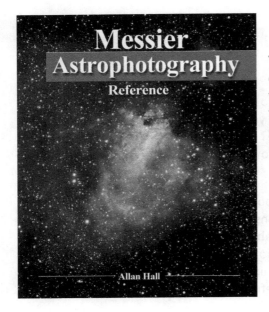

You decide that you want to take images of celestial targets, but need a little help with the targets? This book discusses all 110 Messier targets and includes descriptions, realistic images of each target, star charts and shoot notes to help you image all 110 of the objects yourself.

http://www.allans-stuff.com/mar/

If you have ever wanted to view the wondrous objects of our solar system and beyond, here is the how-to manual to get you well on your way. From purchasing your first telescope, through setting it up and finding objects, to viewing your first galaxy, this book contains everything you need. Learn how to read star maps and navigate the celestial sphere and much more with plenty of pictures, diagrams and charts to make it easy. Written specifically for the novice and assuming the reader has no knowledge of astronomy makes sure that all topics are explained thoroughly from the ground up. Use this book to

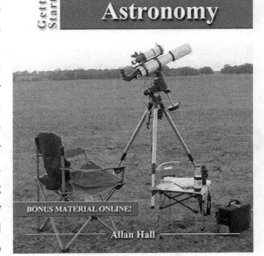

embark on a fantastic new hobby and learn about the universe at the same time!

http://www.allans-stuff.com/va/

WordPress For Normal People

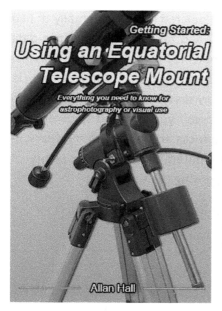

Many midrange and high end telescopes come on equatorial mounts. These mounts are fantastic for tracking celestial objects. Someone who wanted to take pictures of objects in the night sky might even say they are required for all but the most basic astrophotography. The problem is that they can also be unintuitive and require some knowledge to use.

If you have ever struggled to figure out how to use an equatorial telescope mount, this is the book you always wished you had.

http://www.allans-stuff.com/eq/

So you've decided to write a book and get into non-fiction publishing. Now you find yourself faced with the seemingly infinitely harder second step – actually bringing the idea to market. In today's brave new world of self-publishing and open creative markets, it is both an inviting and potentially intimidating arena for authors hoping to turn their non-fiction books into a meaningful source of income. This is a daunting task because it involves a blend of several disciplines that aren't necessarily part of an author's quiver of arrows. Most crucial among these are marketing and digital publishing, each of which requires fluency in fields that authors may or may not have experience in.

http://www.allans-stuff.com/ck/

If you have ever deleted a file accidentally or had a hard drive fail and take all your precious data with then this book is for you. From the simplest procedures of restoring files from your recycle bin to completely disassembling a hard drive to replace a bad head, you will find it covered in here. Tips and tricks from over thirty years of working on computers are here with plenty of images accompanying the text.

http://www.allans-stuff.com/dr/

NOTES:

NOTES:

www.ingramcontent.com/pod-product-compliance
Lightning Source LLC
Chambersburg PA
CBHW062105050326
40690CB00016B/3213